DRY FLY
STRATEGIES

DRY FLY STRATEGIES

PAUL WEAMER

STACKPOLE BOOKS

Guilford, Connecticut

Published by Stackpole Books
An imprint of The Rowman & Littlefield Publishing Group, Inc.
4501 Forbes Blvd., Ste. 200
Lanham, MD 20706
www.rowman.com

Distributed by NATIONAL BOOK NETWORK

British Library Cataloguing in Publication Information available

Library of Congress Cataloging-in-Publication Data

Names: Weamer, Paul, author.
Title: Dry-fly strategies / Paul Weamer.
Description: Guilford, Connecticut : Stackpole Books, [2021] | Includes
   bibliographical references and index. | Summary: "In this
   straightforward book, Paul Weamer breaks down the best methods, rigs,
   and fly patterns to catch more fish"— Provided by publisher.
Identifiers: LCCN 2021004594 (print) | LCCN 2021004595 (ebook) | ISBN
   9780811739535 (hardback) | ISBN 9780811769525 (epub)
Subjects: LCSH: Trout fishing. | Fly fishing.
Classification: LCC SH687 .W39 2021 (print) | LCC SH687 (ebook) | DDC
   799.17/57—dc23
LC record available at https://lccn.loc.gov/2021004594
LC ebook record available at https://lccn.loc.gov/2021004595

For my father, Ed Weamer . . .
a dry-fly purist with a soft spot for
Green Weenies and Frittery Darts

CONTENTS

ACKNOWLEDGMENTS

Thanks to Orvis, Simms, and Regal Engineering; Ross Purnell and *Fly Fisherman* magazine; Jay Nichols and Stackpole Books; Tony Gehman and the TCO Fly Shop; Joe Fox and the Dette Fly Shop; Ed Jaworowski for allowing me to use the photos from one of our fishing trips; Jim Downes for the wonderful cane rod; the amazing Amie Huber; Steve Huber, Jimmy Mincin, Eric Orr, and Bill Ratchford; my wife, Ruthann, and Blue-Winged "Olive," our English mastiff.

And thanks to Charles R. Meck. My friend Charlie passed away on September 18, 2018. I thought of him often while writing this book.

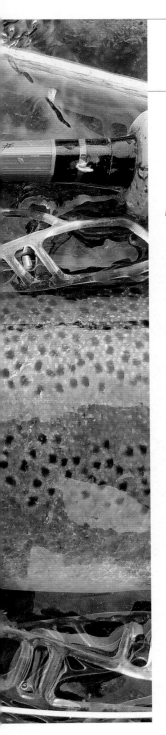

INTRODUCTION

There was a time when many anglers considered dry-fly fishing to be the only real way to fly fish. An English fly-fishing pioneer named Frederick Halford even created a series of rules for the proper way for a gentleman fly fisher to proceed: only cast upstream, only cast to fish that are already rising, and so on. Eventually, a counter opinion rose from another Englishman named G. E. M. Skues. Skues professed the virtues of fishing with sinking flies (nymphs), and these two angling giants had a competitive running discourse in the angling literature at the time.

Most modern anglers don't really care about a supposed proper way to fly fish—and that's not necessarily a bad thing—though there are still places like California's Hot Creek Ranch where you're allowed to fish only with dry flies. All fly fishing is fun, and I really enjoy fishing with nymphs. But if you want to be a complete fly fisherman, you need to know how to catch trout with every method available. And that includes dry flies.

Dry-fly fishing has fallen to a distant third place, behind nymphs and streamers, for many modern anglers. Some of these fishermen won't use dries at all. Structured competitive fly fishing and the rise of Euro-nymphing techniques are now our sport's most

The beauty of a finely crafted bamboo fly rod seems to match the poetry of a wild, brightly colored trout rising to eat a dry fly. For many of today's anglers, dry-fly fishing harkens back to a time when fly fishing was a more contemplative and traditional pursuit.

vocal driving force. After all, there's an oft-repeated adage that trout spend 80 to 90 percent of the time feeding subsurface. So why bother with dry flies if the fish usually won't eat them?

Fly fishing, like most human pursuits, is susceptible to trends. Twenty years ago it seemed like every magazine article was about simplifying the sport, paring down to the essential items. But that has also changed in recent years. Fly fishing is now trending toward complexity, with an abundance of books, videos, and articles discussing an ever-increasing number of better leader formulas and materials, new gadgets, new flies, new equipment, and new methods often invented to comply with competitive fly-fishing rules. Again, there's nothing wrong with this approach. I have a great deal of respect for the level of ingenuity and creativity found in many of today's competitive anglers. And I sometimes use the techniques and flies that these anglers develop and promote. But dry-fly fishing has been largely ignored in this arena in an effort to catch and score as many fish as quickly as possible.

Nearly a decade ago, I was asked to assist my friend George Daniel in

his role as coach of the United States Youth Fly Fishing Team. The kids were participating in a series of skills sessions intended to make them better fly fishermen and to help George pick which anglers would make the team. George asked me to give a streamside seminar about dry-fly fishing, but it was obvious to me, pretty quickly, that the kids weren't really into it. I had a hard time keeping their attention as they tried to listen more closely to other instructors nearby teaching nymphing tactics. These kids didn't care about becoming complete fishermen. They really just wanted to be better competitors, and

Dry-fly master Charlie Meck hooks a large trout that was rising to terrestrials on one of his favorite Pennsylvania spring creeks. Charlie's passing in 2018 was a great loss, but his spirit lives on through his many books about fly fishing and aquatic insects.

they knew that meant nymph fishing. Anglers almost always fish subsurface during competitions, so why bother with dry flies?

But so much of fly fishing's art, science, tradition, and beauty is lost when you ignore rising trout to continue nymphing, even if you're catching fish. And there are times, especially during intense aquatic insect hatches, that you might not catch many fish if you ignore the ones surface feeding in front of you. For most anglers, the only fly-fishing competition in which they'll participate is between themselves and the trout. And if you really want to be competitive, I believe that dry-fly fishing is often the only true way to know how good you've become.

The nymph fisherman's goal, at its core, is simple compared to fishing dry flies during an aquatic insect emergence. Nymph fishermen are trying to catch fish by imitating only one insect life stage—the nymph or larval form. But dry-fly fishing is much more complex when you're trying to imitate emergers, subadults, adults, egg layers, and spent insects, sometimes with overlapping hatches occurring simultaneously. Except during less common occasions when an obvious trout allows you to sight-fish nymphs, wets, or streamers, you cannot fully gauge your skill level while fishing subsurface. Sure, you may have caught 20 fish nymphing a riffle while your friend only caught 4, but maybe there were 200 in there.

You always know where you rank with a rising trout. Were you able to catch it? Did you get a refusal? Did the fish keep rising after the refusal? Or did your poor casting or mending abilities cause the fish to stop rising? If you caught the trout you targeted, you were a great angler for that one fish. But did you catch the next rising fish you found? If you didn't, you need to improve as an angler. And none of us catches every rising trout. There's an old saying: if a trout rises twice in the same spot, it should be caught. Every time. And if there's more magic to be found while fly fishing than watching a wild trout rise to meet your fly at the surface, I've never seen it.

A couple years before my wife and I moved to Montana, my friend Joe Fox (owner of the Dette Fly Shop in Livingston Manor, New York) and I were invited to fish the DeBruce Fly Fishing Club by member John Checchia. The club's water contains a revered pool formed at the junction of the Mongaup and Willowemoc Creeks where angling legend George LaBranche is supposed to have cast the first dry fly in North America. None of the trout living there that day ate our dry flies. But the point is that such a place exists in dry-fly fishing lore. There has to be a spot where an angler cast the first nymph in North America, but I've never heard of it. No one thought it was important enough to write it down.

This book is intended for those who want to become better, more complete anglers by understanding how to fish dry flies. It's written mostly for dry-fly beginners and intermediates, but I hope that even more experienced dry-fly enthusiasts can find some value in these pages. No two fly fishers do everything the same way, and perhaps my methods and experiences will encourage you to think differently about how you fish dry flies as you pursue your own path.

At the beginning of each chapter, I list several crucial skills for you to focus on. Keep these in mind as you read through the text, because it's these

Joe Fox and John Checchia committed heresy by catching a beautiful wild brown trout on a nymph from the mythic pool where George LaBranche claimed to catch the first trout in North America on a dry fly. There are times when a trout that won't eat a dry fly will readily accept a nymph. The most successful fly fishers give the trout what they want to eat.

areas of improvement that will quickly make you a better dry-fly fisherman. In chapter 1, I briefly define dry flies and then examine the best times to use them, using seasonality differences and weather as boundaries. I end the chapter with an examination of dry-fly fishing after dark, an oft-neglected facet of the sport.

Chapter 2 discusses mayflies and their monumental importance to dry-fly fishing. I discuss their life cycle and give a few examples of important features for a few species. But it's not this book's intention to be an aquatic insect guide. My previous book, *The Bug Book*, examines specific aquatic insects more closely. *Dry-Fly Strategies for Trout* is more heavily slanted toward the fly pattern styles that you'll use to imitate insects. But I have included some very good aquatic insect resources in the back of this book, in the Selected Reading section, if you want to learn more about specific insects that are important in your region. Chapter 2 also gives thoughts on the controversial subjects of exact insect color imitation and the importance of hatch charts. I close the chapter with an examination of the common dry-fly pattern styles that you'll find in most fly shops and on retail websites. Understanding how

Trout can often be found rising to dry flies during unpleasant weather. Michael Edwards's persistence during this early spring snowstorm was rewarded with wild trout surface feeding to *Baetis* mayflies.

these flies compare to one another is the key to knowing which dry fly to tie to your leader.

Chapter 3 looks at all the other insects—caddisflies, stoneflies, midges, terrestrials, and others—that bring fish to the surface when they're not eating mayflies. I discuss the most relevant fly pattern styles for these insects as well. Chapter 4 takes the information from chapters 2 and 3 and puts it to practical use by helping you choose the best fly pattern style for a specific rising fish. It includes charts to help guide your fly choice by looking at the various purposes for each fly pattern style in the previous chapters. It also examines the most common attractor dry-fly styles for catching trout on the surface when you aren't finding rising fish. It's vital to be able to read the water when fishing attractor dries, and chapter 4 will tell you how to do that, too.

Chapter 5 is dedicated to dry-fly fishing pace. Pace is one of the most important fly-fishing skills that you can learn, and yet it's often overlooked. Thinking about your pace will guide you to conceptualize what you're really trying to accomplish with your time dry-fly fishing. It will help you understand when you should leave a rising fish and when you should stay and work harder to catch it. The chapter also provides insight into gridding the water to more effectively find receptive fish when you're blind casting dry flies. The chapter ends by looking at your posture to help you gain the advantage on a rising trout.

Chapter 6 discusses the most important casting skills to help you present your dry flies in a more lifelike manner. It focuses on reducing drag, which otherwise may cause a fish to quickly disregard your fly. And it looks at the way in which your position, relative to your rising target, can be improved. Chapter 7 is about decoding the fish we often want to catch the most: large trout, difficult trout, and trout that rise at irregular intervals. After you get your fill of the easy ones, it's these trout that often keep dry-fly anglers engrossed for the long term. I end the chapter with a plan of attack for a rising trout, taking you through the steps I follow from my first cast to a rising fish until I catch it or decide to move on.

The final chapter provides my thoughts on the best tackle for dry-fly fishing. Rods, reels, fly lines, leaders, and tippets are all discussed. I also detail a few of the accessories that are most important for keeping your flies floating. After all, if the flies sink, then you're not really fishing with dry flies, right?

1

Preparation

CRUCIAL POINTS
- Changing seasons have a tremendous impact on dry-fly fishing.
- Weather conditions can improve or hinder dry-fly fishing.
- Trout still eat dry flies after dark.

What is a dry fly? This seems like a simple question, but the answer is nuanced. Is a fly considered dry only if the whole thing floats? What if a portion of the fly sinks, or even if most of it sinks—is it still a dry fly then? I call any fly where at least some portion of the pattern extends above the water's surface a dry fly. For me, dry-fly fishing is conducted when you can see a fish taking something from the water's surface, whether you've identified the fish after it has already risen or you see it for the first time when it rises to eat your fly. It's the visual act of a trout rising to eat something that's outside its realm, above the water, that creates dry-fly fishing. The dry fly could be an emerger, where all of the fly except for the wing sinks. Or it could be a Catskill-style dry, where every bit of the fly is intended to ride upon the water's surface.

Traditional dry flies are tied with materials intended to help them float. But adding floatant to some flies that were originally designed to sink can transform these flies into dry flies. I call these patterns damp flies. This won't work with every nymph. Patterns with bead heads or those with heavy lead wire underbodies will not float no matter how much floatant is applied.

Soft-hackled wet flies, Gary LaFontaine's unweighted Sparkle Pupas, unweighted nymph patterns, and many other flies designed to be fished sub-surface can be treated with fly floatant to make them float, turning them into dry flies, at least for a couple of casts, before they'll need to be dried and have floatant reapplied. Sometimes presenting the fish with something different than what other anglers are casting to them can make a difference. And the buggy appearance from a floating soft-hackle can sometimes be the catalyst for catching a rising fish.

I began experimenting with these damp flies many years ago on the Upper Delaware River. I found that they worked so well on this heavily pressured water that I began calling any damp fly "the secret fly." My friend Ron "Curley" Huber and I had a great time telling our other friends that we were using the secret fly whenever we used damp flies to catch rising trout and they were struggling. Of course, I eventually told everyone what I was doing . . . after getting a few fish and watching the other guys squirm for a bit.

The point is to not limit your thinking about what to use when you're trying to catch a rising fish. Look at all the flies in your boxes as tools to get the job done. Throughout this book, particularly in chapter 8's thoughts on equipment, I spend a lot of time trying to simplify things by using fewer gadgets and gear than many anglers prescribe today. But that changes when it comes to my fly selections. There are few anglers who carry more dry flies with them than I do. And some friends think I make pattern selection over-complicated. But I want as many dry-fly options available to me as possible. I don't want to fail to catch a trout because I don't have the right dry fly.

Do you have to carry hundreds of dry flies with you to catch fish? No. But no one has ever failed to catch a rising trout because they had a lot of dry flies with them. And there's no worse feeling than being surrounded by surface-feeding trout that have just refused the last dry-fly option in your box. There's a great line from Clint Eastwood's *Unforgiven,* "I don't want to get killed from a lack of being able to shoot back." That's how I feel about my dry-fly selection.

DRY-FLY SEASONS

Dry-fly fishing can be productive any time of the year when there are enough insects appearing on the water's surface to inspire the trout to look upward to feed. But some seasons generally provide more dry-fly action than others. Below is a guide to how I perceive the dry-fly seasons, east and west, throughout the angling year.

Spring

Spring is often considered the best season for eastern dry-fly anglers. It's the time when most of the famous eastern hatches appear—Hendricksons (*Ephemerella subvaria*), Grannom Caddis (*Brachycentrus* spp.), Sulphurs (*Ephemerella invaria*), Green Drakes (*Ephemera guttulata*), and many others. Springtime usually brings pleasant temperatures to the East, as well as the year's best streamflows as melting snow and spring rains recharge aquifers, providing lots of water for fish and fishermen. Morning dry-fly fishing may be slow in the spring, depending on air temperatures at night. But springtime trout are usually easier to catch, from late morning through the afternoon, as higher streamflows, combined with increasing water

Matt Grobe illustrates that springtime in the East, and pre-runoff in the West, provides some of the best opportunities to find large trout eating dry flies. The fish are often less wary after a winter of reduced angling pressure.

temperatures, make them feed more aggressively than they did during the winter months.

The fish are also generally less wary at this time due to the reduced angling pressure in the previous months, though this changes quickly as spring progresses. Winter has ended. The days are getting longer. Birds are migrating back to the rivers and streams. Flowers are blooming. Mayfly, caddisfly, and stonefly hatches are just beginning to appear. The whole season lies before you. And trout can sometimes be found rising nearly all day long. Life is good for eastern dry-fly fishermen in the spring.

But springtime is different in the West. The western United States is a big place. So there is a great deal of geographical variation that impacts fly fishermen. And spring can often be a great time to be a dry-fly fisherman in the Desert Southwest and other areas. But in the Rocky Mountains region, where some of our country's greatest trout fisheries emanate, spring can be more difficult.

There is usually a brief springtime period in the Rockies when winter is ending and warming air temperatures bring good to great dry-fly fishing. However, the warm air that is slowly increasing water temperature, and thereby instigating aquatic insect hatches, is also beginning to melt the mountain snowpack, inducing runoff. Western high-mountain runoff is a double-edged sword. It's the vast mountain snow reservoir that keeps many rivers and streams charged with cold water throughout the summer. But at its peak, runoff will make many trout fisheries unfishable due to high, cold, and sometimes dangerous flows.

I live in the Yellowstone River's drainage. Here, good springtime dry-fly fishing ends with our best caddis hatch, the Mother's Day Caddis. Dry-fly anglers can usually get a few days to a week of good fishing before our rivers and their tributaries become entirely unfishable from heavy runoff. And this unfishable period can last from the beginning of May until sometime in July.

There are exceptions outside the Yellowstone region. Tailwaters—rivers that flow from a dam, like the Missouri and Bighorn—can mitigate runoff some years and extend good spring fly fishing. However, flood control and other water-management requirements can cause high flows on these fisheries, too, creating difficult

to impossible dry-fly fishing. But what many western trout fisheries lose in springtime dry-fly action, they gain during the summer.

Summer

Summer dry-fly fishing in the East is often much more difficult than during the spring. River and stream flows usually drop significantly without being fed from high mountain snows as they are in the Rocky Mountain West. The low water can become too warm for trout preferences (approximately 55 to 65 degrees) during the middle of the day, so the best dry-fly fishing is now

Leaving your waders at home and wet wading during the summer months can be a great way to fish, as long as the water you are fishing is clean. But low water levels and daytime heat can sometimes force anglers to fish early in the morning or closer to dark, when water temperatures are more ideally suited for trout preferences.

often found at daybreak and in the late evening, just before dark. Fish have been heavily pressured during the intense spring fishing season, and they are now often more difficult to catch because of it.

Excellent eastern hatches will still occur during the summer—Tricos (*Tricorythodes* spp.) and various Cahill mayfly species, Isos (*Isonychia* spp.), various caddis species, and others—but the fishing is often compressed into brief periods before and after the middle of the day's heat. Terrestrials become very important during daytime fishing for eastern dry-fly anglers. Ants, beetles, and a myriad of other land-born insects will catch fish on the surface. But water temperature is often a concern for ethical catch-and-release anglers on some of the East's fabled wild trout streams in the summer. You shouldn't try to catch the fish that might rise to your dry-fly patterns as water temperatures climb toward 70 degrees because the struggle to get them into your net will almost certainly kill them.

But the East is also a big place. There are spring creeks that ooze from the ground with much colder water temperatures than most freestone streams, as well as tailwaters that receive their water from releases at the bottom of deep, cold reservoirs, which can keep eastern anglers fishing to rising trout all summer long.

Summer often brings the opposite conditions for western anglers in the drainages along the Rocky Mountains. The raging runoff period is now diminishing, and that coincides with the famous Salmon Fly (*Pteronarcys* spp.) hatch in some waterways, though this hatch sometimes occurs when the water is still too high to fish. And it doesn't exist in every river and stream. But as the waters recede, other western summer hatches bring fish to the surface. Caddis appear in great abundance on most trout waters. Pale Morning Duns (*Ephemerella* spp.), Western Green Drakes (*Drunella* spp.), and Tricos (*Tricorythodes* spp.) emerge in many waters. Terrestrials also play a vital role for western dry-fly anglers. Cicadas, moths, and epic grasshopper fishing draw anglers from all over the world. High mountain streams, where the elevation ensures that temperatures will remain cold at night and cool during the day, can host rising trout all day long during the summer.

The summer dry-fly fishing can be so good in the West that many eastern anglers leave their own good fishing to travel to western trout fisheries. I spent over 10 years owning and managing fly shops along the Upper Delaware River, and we would joke about the great exodus my customers would make during the summer. Parking areas that were overflowing in the spring would see far fewer anglers, even though the Delaware's cold water releases, and the heavy summer Sulphur hatches they instigated, created great dry-fly fishing most years.

But western trout fisheries aren't completely immune to their own weather-related difficulties during the summer. Years with poor snowpack and the heat's impact on lower-elevation rivers and streams can still cause some trout fisheries to suffer from the effects of warm summer water. Montana, my current home state, will sometimes implement "hoot owl" restrictions during the summer, which prohibit fishing during the hottest part of the day to protect trout from thermal stress. Montana will even close rivers entirely during particularly hot and dry summers. Severe weather can impact western trout fisheries, too. Summer afternoon thunderstorms are common in many places in the West. These deluges can shut down the fishing for an evening, or even a couple of days, if the rain is heavy enough to muddy the water.

Fall

Fall usually brings cooler air and water temperatures to eastern trout streams that have been baking with high heat and humidity during the summer months. The days are getting shorter and the sun is less intense. Angling pressure is diminishing because free time is less available for many anglers, as their vacations have ended for the year. Some fly fishermen focus on hunting in the fall or move on to other outdoor activities. The river and stream flows usually remain very low, but the low water can concentrate the trout, making them easier to find. Low water can also encourage the fish to rise more freely to attractor dry flies. In spite of the low fall waterflows, trout usually become a little easier to catch as angler activity dwindles and cooler water temperature inspires the fish to feed more aggressively as winter approaches.

Daytime hatches become more common in the fall. Slate Drakes (*Isonychia* spp.), Blue-Winged Olives (*Baetis* spp.), October Caddis (*Pycnopsyche* sp.), and other aquatic insects will bring fish to the surface. Flying ants usually swarm sometime beginning in mid to late August and can appear any time after that until the first or second hard frost. Remnants of hurricanes and tropical storms sometimes bring a heavy rain to eastern fisheries as they travel north this time of year, recharging streams and occasionally forcing them to flood stage.

The fall fishing in the West is similar to the East with fewer fishermen vying for the attention of increasingly more aggressive trout. River and stream levels are usually getting low in the West this time of year, too, as the high mountain snow reservoirs begin to run out of water. Weather can become very undependable during the fall in the Mountain West. It may be 60 degrees today but snowing tomorrow, and this is particularly true for high-elevation streams. Some western trout fisheries like those found in Yellowstone National Park close for the winter.

Aquatic insect hatches will still occur, particularly in late summer/early fall, and they can bring fish to the surface during the day. Blue-Winged Olives (*Baetis* spp.), the last of the Green Drakes (*Drunella* and *Timpanoga* spp.), various caddis species, and others can inspire the trout to rise. But fall is often a time to search with attractor fly patterns. Fish become less likely to take another grasshopper imitation after hordes of anglers have been hooking them with the flies for months. A small ant or beetle imitation is usually a much better bet this time of year. Humpies, small stimulators, Royal Wulffs, Patriots, and other general attractor flies will often catch more fish than exact hatch-matching patterns that the fish saw all summer.

Cool air and water temperatures, and the threat of a long hard winter, often instigate trout to surface feed in the fall. Autumn is the favorite season of many dry-fly anglers, in spite of low-water conditions that can make the trout wary.

Winter

Winter is usually the slowest season of the year for dedicated dry-fly fishermen. Many freestone fisheries in the East and West will freeze over, ending all fly fishing until warmer weather returns. Aquatic insect hatches for mayflies, caddisflies, and stoneflies are usually nonexistent in midwinter. And the cold river and stream flows will often discourage trout from rising even if there are insects on the water's surface. But there are wintertime exceptions.

Both eastern and western spring creeks and tailwaters can host midge and Blue-Winged Olive (*Baetis* spp.) hatches that range from very sparse to extremely heavy in early and late winter. Again, the cold water temperatures that slow trout metabolism can impact the fish's willingness to surface feed, but it's not uncommon to find trout rising during warmer winter afternoons. The window to find rising fish is heavily tied to warming water temperature, even a degree or two, and most often occurs late morning through early afternoon.

Trout and aquatic insects are usually most active when water temperatures are moving toward the 55 to 65 degree mark. That means that if the water temperature increases from 33 degrees in the morning to 35 at lunch, there's a chance that this temperature change will motivate bugs to hatch and fish to rise. But if a cold front moves in and the water temperature drops during the day, fish and aquatic insect activity usually decrease, too. On warmer winter days, melting snow, running into the water, can also drop stream temperatures, creating a fishing lull. You should usually expect dry-fly fishing to be nonexistent, east and west, for significant portions of the winter months. But this isn't true everywhere.

Our great southern climate trout fisheries, east and west, can be the exception to slow winter dry-fly action. While many of these fisheries are stocked

Frigid temperatures and ice severely limit dry-fly fishing opportunities in most northern freestone trout waters from early to midwinter. But by late winter, when flowing water reappears, you may find the first rising trout of the year, often eating midges.

with hatchery trout because they warm too much in the summer for fish survival, there are a surprising number of wild trout here, too. Mountain streams where the elevation keeps the water cool in the summer and tailwaters that flow from bottom-release dams create excellent wild trout fisheries throughout the South.

My good friend and mentor, Charlie Meck, used to spend his winters far from his Pennsylvania home, in Arizona. Charlie and I would talk on the telephone throughout the winter, and one of the things he liked to talk about the most was the terrific Trico (*Tricorythodes* spp.) fishing he'd pursue in Arizona's Salt River. The diminutive Trico mayflies are a summer hatch in northern climates, both east and west. But the much warmer Arizona weather induced them to hatch during the winter months. Charlie would experience great Arizona dry-fly fishing every January while I was freezing somewhere in the North.

WEATHER

When we're discussing the best seasons for dry-fly fishing, what we're really talking about is the predominant weather that usually happens at that time of year. Dry-fly fishing is more susceptible to the whims of nature than nymph fishing. Trout are always under the water and they're usually eating while they're there. But they won't always rise to a dry fly. There are times when fish are more prone to surface feed and others when you're better off planning to nymph. But it can sometimes be difficult to know when these times will occur. The trout on some occasions, due to reasons only they know, unexpectedly rise when conditions are less than ideal. And there are other times when the water is covered with aquatic insects and you can't find a rising fish on the whole stream.

Over the years, I've found that some weather patterns increase or decrease my chances of finding rising trout. But you must also take account of the

Dry-fly anglers often expect midge, or small Blue-Winged Olive, hatches to be a possibility when there's snow on the ground. But early spring stoneflies and other insects may also appear, like this large caddis standing on a late fall snowbank.

time of year when these conditions occur by using weather suggestions in conjunction with the seasonal factors I've already discussed. For instance, a day with rainy drizzle in the spring will usually produce much better dry-fly action than if that same weather occurred in the winter. Aquatic or terrestrial insects need to have been recently present, most of the time, for fish to look toward the surface to feed. And you're much more likely to find insects in the spring, summer, and fall than in winter.

Best Times to Find Surface-Feeding Trout

Overcast Days: Trout are very sensitive to light. They don't have eyelids and they must look into the sun as they rise to take a dry fly. An overcast day seems to make the trout feel a little safer from overhead predators, too.

Drizzling Rain: It's not a surprise to most experienced anglers that trout like to feed during the rain. But I've heard many new anglers express how good they expect the fishing to be when it's bright and sunny, pleasant for humans but not necessarily trout. Remember, the trout are already wet. The weather that's most comfortable for you to be fishing in isn't always ideal for them. But know that rain intensity matters, too. A light drizzle is usually much better for finding rising trout than a hard, driving rain that disturbs the water's surface, making it more difficult for fish to see the insects on it.

Gently Falling Snow: When you encounter a winter's day on a stream with midge or Blue-Winged Olive hatches, the snow seems to get the fish looking toward the surface to feed. This may also be due to the fact that if it's snowing, it's cloudy. But I've also wondered if the snow falling gently to the water's surface doesn't instigate the fish to focus on what's happening above them.

Electrical Storms: I have found fish rising heavily, many times, during the initial stages of a thunderstorm. Perhaps it's because the sky is darkening, making it easier for the fish to look toward the surface and encouraging aquatic insects to hatch. Maybe it's a drop in air and water temperature or due to barometric reasons. But trout seem to rise best as a storm moves into an area or just briefly after it ends. Once it starts raining with full force or the sun returns, fishing usually slows down. There is a danger factor to consider while fishing during lightning, and you really shouldn't do it if the lightning is close. I remember an afternoon storm on the Lower East Branch of the Delaware River many years ago that instigated seemingly every fish in the river to rise when nothing was happening a few minutes before the storm approached. I foolishly stood in the middle of the river, risking my life with lightning crashing all around me, uttering, "One more cast. Just one more cast." I'm older and smarter than that now.

Calm Winds or a Gentle Breeze: Wind is a concern for dry-fly fishermen for many reasons, the biggest being that it makes it really difficult to

A light drizzle can make some anglers decide to stay home. But the trout are already wet, so they don't mind. The humid air makes it difficult for aquatic insects to fly from the water, creating easy meals for the fish, and often instigating excellent dry-fly opportunities. (Photo by Ruthann Weamer)

cast accurately. But strong wind also disturbs the water's surface, sometimes inhibiting trout from easily seeing small aquatic insects they might otherwise eat. On the other hand, a gentle breeze can sometimes ruffle the surface just enough to obscure an angler, their imprecise casts, and their leader and tippet, making the fish a little easier to catch.

Worst Times to Expect Surface-Feeding Trout

Bright and Sunny: Sunny days can sometimes provide good dry-fly fishing, especially in the winter or early spring, when the sun increases water temperature enough to affect trout metabolism or to instigate aquatic insect hatches. But it's just as likely, throughout the rest of the year, that few aquatic insects will hatch in the bright sun, and fish will be less inclined to surface feed if they do.

Hot Days: An extended period of sunny, hot weather in the late spring, fall, or (most often) summer can raise water temperatures to the point where both trout and aquatic insects are active only during the coolest part of the day: first thing in the morning, the last hour leading into sunset, and throughout the night. The fabled Eastern Green Drake (*Ephemera guttulata*) hatch is famous for this. Some years, you'll find hundreds of spinners (often called coffin flies) in streamside vegetation while seeing very few duns hatch. That's because warm weather is making the flies emerge after dark. Terrestrials can be an exception to this rule. The land-based insects often become more active during warm weather, which increases the chances they'll fly, hop, or fall into the water where a trout is waiting. Look for fish in areas of shade along the banks when this happens.

Heavy Rain/Heavy Snow: Whereas a light drizzle or snow flurries can make for great dry-fly fishing, heavy rain and snow usually create poor dry-fly conditions. The trout can't see the bugs on the surface. The angler can't see the trout's riseforms. And it's nearly impossible to keep your flies floating when they are getting drenched from above and below.

Gusting Wind: A forceful, gusting wind disturbs the water's surface and seems to make it more difficult for trout to see insects and definitely makes it more difficult for anglers to see riseforms. I've experienced many days where trout would rise only during the brief moments between wind gusts. These days can be very frustrating. If the wind is steadily blowing enough to roil the water without pausing, it's usually better to nymph.

DRY-FLY FISHING AT NIGHT

The best summertime dry-fly fishing can sometimes occur after dark, as elevated water temperatures, combined with low water and bright sunshine, keep the fish hiding during the day. A lot of anglers don't like to fish after dark. It can be sort of spooky if you're by yourself. Bats are flying around. Wild animals are more active. One of the reasons that many anglers enjoy dry-fly fishing is because it's visual; there's nothing quite as exciting as watching a big fish rise to take your dry fly. And you probably won't see the fish take your fly after the sun sets. In spite of this, dry-fly fishing at night can also be a great deal of fun and very productive.

It's usually ideal to be streamside the last hour before dark, while the sun is still setting, if you're planning to fish into the night. Most anglers will be leaving the water, and you may be able to procure the best water all to yourself. Fish will often begin to feed at this time, so you may have targets right away, but it's also a good idea to be able to see the water you'll be fishing at night before the sun sets. You'll want to take notice of obstructions, like overhanging tree limbs where you can tangle your fly, or dangerous areas like unusually deep holes that can be impossible to see while wading after dark. That's why it's generally best to night fish only in sections that you have fished extensively during the day.

Trout will be much less skittish after dark and that gives you a few advantages. First, you can generally wade much closer to rising fish without scaring them as long as you move very slowly. Listen for the sounds of fish slurping flies from the surface and then slowly move that direction. Often, you can get close enough to see the fish rising from the glow of starlight or the moon. Choose calmer water in a pool, or the tail of a pool, to begin searching for fish. It's much more difficult to hear and see trout rising after dark in a riffle or broken water.

You should shorten your leader for fishing after dark. It'll be easier to know where your fly is landing if you're using a short leader. But you don't want to cut your leader so short that you don't get a good drift—that can still be very important at night. By trimming your leader, you'll also be using heavier tippet. I almost never use tippet lighter than 4X, tied to a 7½-foot leader when fishing after dark. And that's a good thing because some-

times very large fish feed once the sun sets. The heavier tippet means that you may also be able to retrieve your fly, rather than breaking if off, if you catch some brush.

Fly patterns can often be larger during the night than during the day. You don't want to use a fly so big that the trout will ignore it. But choosing a pattern one to two sizes larger than the naturals can work well if there's a hatch. I especially like to use oversize flies if the trout are feeding on a heavy emergence or spinnerfall and the water is covered with naturals. It's one way to make your fly obvious to the fish when they have so many from which to

Sunny, cloudless skies combined with low water and heavy angling pressure can reduce daytime dry-fly opportunities, particularly during the summer months. It is usually more productive to fish a riffle when rising trout are not evident in the slow pools.

choose. And sometimes that's the key to getting the trout to eat your fly rather than the natural floating beside it.

I typically use a brightly colored, or highly visible, dry like a White Wulff because some nights I can see it. Often, mayflies that hatch during summer nights are lightly colored anyway. And trout don't seem to be able to discern between shades of color at night nearly as well as they can during the day.

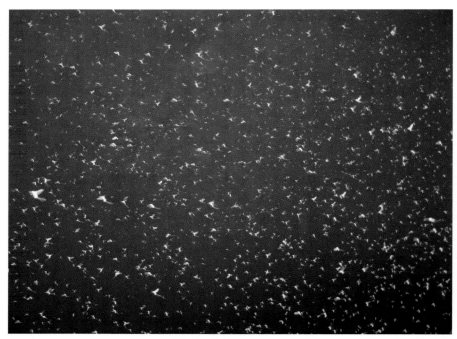

Many aquatic insect hatches and mating flights occur right before, and after, dark during the summer months due to elevated air and water temperatures. Savvy dry-fly fisherman will often arrive streamside an hour before dark to partake in the action while many other anglers are heading home.

You should have a light with you, but try to not use it. Artificial light on the water may frighten the fish, and you'll ruin your already limited vision for a period of time after you turn on the light. Once you locate a rising fish and move as close as you can without disturbing it, it's time to cast. Cast about a foot upstream of the rise and let your fly float to the fish. If you hear the fish feed or see movement near where you expect your fly to be floating, lift the rod tip to set the hook. You may do this a few times and realize the fish ate something that wasn't your fly. But the only way to be sure is to set the hook. And every once in a while, they'll be a fish on the end of your line.

2

Flies for Mayflies

CRUCIAL POINTS
- Mayflies are perhaps the most important insects for dry-fly fishing.
- It's not necessary to imitate the exact color of aquatic insects.
- Dry flies can be broken into pattern styles that have unique features for use in varying water types and for imitating insects that emerge in specific ways.

Mayflies are synonymous with dry-fly fishing. They create some of the most famous and sought-after hatches in our sport's mythology. Mayfly species can vary greatly in appearance and the way in which they emerge from nymphs, much more so than caddisflies and stoneflies, many of which look and behave very similar to one another. It's this mayfly variation and complexity that earn them an entire chapter in this book.

THE MAYFLY LIFE CYCLE
When anglers envision a beautiful stream with fish eagerly sipping flies from its surface, they are most often imagining mayflies as a central figure. There's a good reason for this. Mayflies live in rivers, lakes, and streams throughout the world. Even in places like Florida, where water is too warm for viable trout populations, mayflies exist. And most everywhere trout live, they coexist with mayflies.

The mayfly life cycle comprises three stages: nymph, dun (subimago), and spinner (imago). But for fishing purposes, we add another stage called emerger. It's this stage, plus duns and spinners, that are imitated with dry flies. Emergers are actually just duns that have not yet freed themselves from the water. Their now empty, or near empty, nymph skin is called a shuck or a trailing shuck when some of it remains attached to the dun before the process is complete.

Mayflies begin as eggs that are deposited in the water. There are many different mayfly species, and they don't all deposit their eggs in the same way.

Anglers often imagine this happening with waves of spinners flying upstream, the females dipping their abdomens in riffles to release their eggs before falling spent to the surface, ending their lives. And it does occur this way often. But some mayflies actually fly to dry land, beside the stream, and then walk into the water to deposit their eggs. And some drop their eggs from above the water without ever touching it.

Most male mayflies do not die on the water after mating. They simply fly away, leaving the females to finish their life cycle. The exact way in which every fly-fishing-relevant mayfly species concludes its life is beyond this book's scope. But I have included book suggestions in the Selected Reading list for those who want to get a greater understanding of the mayflies that exist in their favorite trout waters.

Once mayfly eggs hatch, they become nymphs. Nymphs are the little creatures that you'll find crawling along the cobbles in stream bottoms if you turn

In healthy fisheries where mayfly populations are robust, trout will sometimes eagerly eat dry flies even when the mayflies aren't hatching. The key is to choose one that looks like something the fish wants to eat. This rainbow trout ate a Parachute Adams, which isn't intended to exactly imitate any real insect, yet looks similar to many.

Gilled mayfly nymphs live in the bottom of rivers, lakes, and streams, waiting for their moment to hatch into winged, air-breathing subadults. It's difficult to believe that this horned, gilled Golden Drake (*Anthopotamus* sp.) nymph will emerge into the beautiful, dainty mayfly dun in the following photo.

Now free from its watery nymphal home, this Golden Drake (*Anthopotamus* sp.) subimago (dun) will rest in streamside vegetation before transforming yet again. All mayfly duns have upright wings and either two or three tails, depending on their species.

This sexually mature Golden Drake (*Anthopotamus* sp.) imago, also known as an adult or spinner, is ready to complete its life cycle. Notice how the wings have turned mostly clear and the body color has also changed. This is a common occurrence when mayflies transform from duns into spinners. The exact changes are particular to species.

Large wild trout like this beautiful brown will not waste calories to surface feed. They will often seek out mayflies that are most vulnerable—newly emerged and not yet ready to fly, crippled, or spent after laying their eggs and unable to leave the water's surface.

over submerged rocks, though some species are burrowers that dig into the substrate. Most of the year, you'll see these nymphs only if you dig into the sand and dirt under the water. They become available to trout, most often, as they prepare to emerge into duns. Mayfly egg and nymph stages do not produce dry-fly fishing opportunities. These stages are imitated only with flies that sink.

At roughly the same time each year, and always in the same order from one species to the next, the nymphs transform beneath their skin, use gases to break the skin open, and transform into what we fly fishers call emergers. Some will emerge on the stream bottom and some just beneath the water's surface or in its uppermost layer, called the surface film. A few species like those found in the *Isonychia* and *Siphlonurus* genera will usually crawl onto streamside rocks or vegetation and emerge, similar to stoneflies, which we'll discuss later. These mayflies don't always provide good dry-fly fishing opportunities during this part of their life cycle because they aren't reachable for trout.

Mayfly duns that emerge in the water (which is most of them) usually float on the water's surface as their wings harden, enabling flight. This process can be delayed by cold weather or rain. Sometimes wind blows the duns onto their sides, trapping one of their wings in the water and creating the mayflies that fishermen call cripples. Anything that keeps the flies on the water for a longer period of time is a benefit for dry-fly fishermen. Trout key in on these insects because their lack of immediate flight capabilities makes them easy targets.

The duns that fly from the water's surface without drowning or getting eaten by fish or birds now find a place to rest and transform again into sexually mature adults that fly anglers call spinners. This transformation happens very quickly for some species—within a couple hours—but for others, it can take days before the transformation is complete.

Most species begin with more males completing their life cycles than females. The males gather over riffles, waiting for females to appear to mate. It's common for anglers to see hundreds of male spinners flying in the evenings and excitement building as they expect mating to occur, instigating the fish to feed in earnest. But sometimes enough females haven't emerged yet for all the males, so most of the male spinners return to the vegetation to wait to try again the next night. This leaves fishermen frustrated because the trout-feeding frenzy they expected to happen fails to materialize.

Many of the males fly away from the water after mating takes place, never reaching the surface. But the females must lay their eggs, and when they do, their life cycle complete, they usually fall spent to the water, often with their wings outstretched, where trout feed upon their lifeless bodies. This often happens in the last hour before dark, during the night, or in the early morning hours, depending on weather conditions. These spinnerfalls create some of the best dry-fly fishing opportunities of the year.

But as important as mayflies are for dry-fly fishing, on any given day, it can be just as important, or even more so, to imitate caddisflies, stoneflies, midges, terrestrials, and other insects, depending on what the trout are eating. Sometimes there are few aquatic insects available to the trout. At other times you may find various life-cycle stages occurring simultaneously for several types of aquatic insects, with one trout choosing one type of insect and another trout selectively feeding on a different one, while a third fish eats everything that floats by its feeding lane. This is what makes dry-fly fishing so challenging and so much fun.

FLY PATTERN COLOR

One of the things you will quickly realize if you have more than one fly shop in your area—or if you order flies from more than one company online, or

These Blue-Winged Olive (*Baetis* sp.) duns, one crippled and the other perfectly formed, were found on the water at the same time. Yet they aren't exactly the same color. Matching the exact natural color of aquatic insects with artificial flies is probably impossible, though some anglers find it fun to try. Thankfully, it's not vital to catch rising trout.

sometimes even if you order flies from different batches from the same fly supplier—is that fly pattern colors can vary, sometimes dramatically, even among the exact same dry fly in the exact same pattern style. For instance, the Blue-Winged Olive Parachutes in one fly shop may be much lighter than the same described pattern from another. This causes some fly fishers a great deal of stress when they try to imitate an aquatic insect's exact coloration. But should it?

A man came into a fly shop I was managing many years ago, and he was upset that he had lots of fish rising around him the night before but couldn't catch any of them. What made it worse was that the man was not alone. There were many other fly fishers there that night and everyone was catching fish except for this poor guy. He told me, "I guess my Sulphur mayfly dries were just too orange."

I asked him if he really believed that, and he said he did. I told him that there may have been many reasons the fish didn't eat his fly, but that I was pretty certain that his fly's color wasn't one of them. "How can you know that?" he responded somewhat angrily. "Do you think every angler was using the exact same color fly last night?" I asked. "Some of them had to have tied their own flies, while others bought them from different places, and yet they all ended up the exact same color?" He just looked at me. I don't think he had considered that.

Of course, those anglers were using many different-colored flies. And it didn't matter. Lots of aquatic insects darken in color after they're exposed to air. Some change to a completely different color after time. So flies hatching right in front of you might be lighter colored than those floating down to you. And insect color can also vary according to what the bugs ate as nymphs or larvae; they might be a shade darker or lighter in one area compared to those emerging up- or downstream.

Creating dubbing colors to try to match exact colors for the insects hatching on your favorite streams can be a lot of fun. And if that makes you feel better prepared, do it. But it's not necessary. I've found that using a similar color shade is much more important than exact color imitation. And the most important factor is probably your fly's size: you usually won't catch many fish if you're casting a size 14 imitation when the trout are eating size 18 insects. In the same vein, I wouldn't use a dark brown fly if the fish are eating yellow bugs. But if your flies are pale yellow, rather than butter yellow, I don't believe the fish will care. Make a good cast with the correct-size fly and get a good drift, and exact fly color won't be the reason you do, or do not, catch fish.

HATCH PROGRESSION VS. HATCH CHARTS

Hatch charts have long been a favorite method of predicting when specific aquatic insects may be found. But in my previous book, *The Bug Book*, I spend a great deal of time expressing why hatch charts aren't really that effective in preparing anglers to find specific aquatic insects on their local waters.

Hatch charts are static tools that cannot take into consideration vital information such as recent weather patterns or the long-term effects of climate change. I have experienced wild timing swings of a month or more for the same hatch, in the same stream. Droughts, floods, and unusual patterns of unseasonably cold or hot weather will all conspire to make a hatch chart one of the most unreliable tools in all of fly fishing. Even streams in the same drainage, but flowing at different elevations, can have significant timing differences in terms of when specific hatches will occur.

The best advice I can give dry-fly anglers hoping to encounter a specific aquatic insect hatch is to follow hatch progression. Hatch progression uses the

Hatch charts are often unreliable because they are static, unable to include up-to-the-minute information like weather and water flows that change from year to year. Hatch progression is a much more reliable way to predict which insects you'll find streamside. For instance, I don't know exactly when the Western Salmonflies (*Pteronarcys* spp.) pictured here will emerge next season, but I do know that they won't appear until sometime after the Mother's Day Caddis (*Brachycentrus* spp.) have appeared.

understanding that though various aquatic insect hatches occur on different dates from one year to the next, they will always follow each other in a specific order as the season progresses. For instance, I cannot forecast when hatches of Eastern Green Drake (*Ephemera guttulata*) mayflies will appear, but I can guarantee that they won't begin hatching until the Hendrickson (*Ephemerella subvaria*) emergences are long gone. In the West, I don't know when the Salmonflies will hatch, but I know that they won't commence until the Mother's Day Grannom Caddis (*Brachycentrus* spp.) emergence is over for the season.

By understanding the order in which mayflies, caddisflies, and stoneflies appear in the waters you fish, you can have a good idea of what to expect when you visit a stream and discover what is currently hatching. But there is a big caveat to this: Not every hatch occurs on every stream. So unless you fish only well-known streams where someone can tell you which hatches have ended and which are coming, you'll have to figure it out for yourself. The only way to do this is to spend as much time streamside as you can and take notes from one year to the next about the insects you find. But trout waters are constantly changing, and a pollution event or an extreme weather event like a flood can have a dramatic influence on the hatches you'll find next year.

COMMON MAYFLY DRY-FLY STYLES

There are many different kinds of dry flies available for fishermen that can all be used to imitate the same hatch. So how do you know which is the best one to choose? In the following section, I break down the most common dry-fly styles by looking at the construction features that make them unique. It's these features, and what they do best, that will help you decide which fly to use. It's impossible to list every possible pattern style because there are so many of them and new ones are being developed all the time. But the lists in this and the following two chapters outline the most common.

Catskill Style

Catskill-style flies originated in New York's Catskill Mountain region and are sometimes also called standard or traditional dry flies. I group these styles

Catskill-style dry flies were developed in New York's Catskill Mountains region, but they will catch trout from coast to coast. The thorax style was developed by Pennsylvania's Vincent Marinaro to produce a dry with a more natural appearance for fishing on slow-moving spring creeks.

together because the flies share the same general shape and are useful in the same ways. Catskill-style flies are most commonly constructed to imitate mayfly duns with sparse hackles, wrapped around the hook shank so the fibers extend perpendicular from it. Tails are made from a single clump of sparse hackle fibers. Wings are usually made by dividing feather fibers from a duck, though divided wings made from two hen hackle tips are also very common. Bodies are either dubbed into a taper using fur or made by wrapping a feather stem (quill) to give the appearance of segmentation. Standard-style flies will often incorporate many Catskill-style elements, like a dubbed body and perpendicular-wrapped hackle, but these flies will often substitute other materials—cul de canard (CDC) feathers for the wings, deer hair for the tail, or many other options. Because Catskill and standard flies have hackle that keeps their bodies off of the water, they are best used in riffles and braided water or to imitate mayfly species that leave the water's surface very quickly once they have hatched into duns. If you omit the wings from a Catskill-style fly and use oversized hackle and a quill body, you have now tied a variant. Variants are designed to float very high on the water, making them an especially good choice for fishing very rough water where many other more flush-floating styles would quickly sink.

Thorax Style

The thorax style was developed by Vincent Marinaro as a way to transform Catskill-style flies into a better option for imitating mayfly duns on the flatter, calmer water that is often found in spring creeks. Thorax-style flies have tails that are divided and usually made from hackle or synthetic fibers like Microfibetts. Microfibetts are synthetic fibers that look like the individual strands of a paintbrush. Bodies are usually dubbed just like Catskill-style flies, but the wing is often made from a single hen hackle feather tip. The most important difference between thorax- and Catskill-style flies is how the hackle is wrapped. Whereas Catskill-style flies place each hackle wrap next to another at a 90-degree angle to the hook shank, the thorax-style hackle is wrapped at a slanted angle, beginning closer to the middle of the hook shank so it stands with an X shape when finished. This attempts to more closely mimic the stance of a natural mayfly dun on the water's surface. Thorax style is often a better option than Catskill style for flat water yet retains good floatation for fishing riffles.

Parachute Style

Parachute-style flies are made with hackle that is wound around a post, parallel to the hook shank, and they work well as imitations for mayfly cripples, duns, spinners, and emergers that sit flush on the water's surface. The parachute post can be constructed from just about anything as long as it floats

A parachute dry fly's horizontal-wound hackle helps the fly ride flush with the water, making it a great choice for fishing flat pools. The Compara-dun style, invented by Al Caucci and Bob Nastasi and popularized in the book *Hatches*, is also an excellent flat-water choice. It's often necessary to show rising trout options: fly patterns that perform similarly on the water but look different.

and is visible enough for anglers to see it. Deer hair, various feathers, and synthetic yarns and foam are all commonly used in post construction. Tails are most often made from feather fibers, hairs, or Microfibetts tied into two or three distinct clumps to imitate mayfly duns. But emergers can also be designed by forming the tail from synthetic yarn to imitate a trailing shuck. Most parachute flies are tied on straight shank hooks, but flies tied on fine-wire, curved hooks like those used for the Klinkhammer are also common. Parachutes are most often used in flat-water applications because they sit low on the water's surface and are easily submerged in rough riffles.

Compara-dun Style

Compara-duns were developed by Al Caucci and Bob Nastasi as an inexpensive, easy-to-tie pattern style made from only three materials: deer hair, dubbing, and Microfibetts. Compara-duns sit flush on the water's surface because they float mainly due to their deer hair wings. This makes them an excellent option for imitating newly emerged mayfly duns that are struggling to fly and spinners that are trapped in the water's surface film. Compara-duns are very durable but can be difficult to see in heavy riffles, and they can sometimes sink more easily than hackled patterns. If you replace the Compara-dun's divided fiber tail with a trailing shuck, made from synthetic materials and colored to match the nymphal case of an emerging mayfly, you have now tied Craig Mathews's Sparkle Dun. Sparkle Duns may appear even more desirable to trout because their trailing shuck suggests an emerging insect that isn't yet able to fly, and that's why I tend to fish Sparkle Duns more often than Compara-duns. Other Compara-dun and Sparkle Dun construction options include substituting CDC feathers or synthetic yarns for the traditional deer hair wings to create a slimmer, more subtle profile, as well as replacing the dubbed body with a quill one made from a hackle stem. Compara-duns and Sparkle Duns are some of my favorite flies for fishing pools and braided water during hatches of mayflies that emerge in or near the surface film.

No-Hackle Style

The No-hackle style was developed by Doug Swisher and Carl Richards to imitate mayfly duns with a very sparsely tied dry fly. Its dominant features are a divided Microfibett tail (just like a Compara-dun), dubbed body, and feather wings that are placed to the sides of the hook shank and usually made from goose slips or other feathers, though synthetic materials are sometimes substituted. No-hackles aren't very buoyant, sinking easily in heavy riffles, and they can be difficult to see on the water. Their wings (when tied from goose slips) are fragile and can become easily shredded after catching multiple trout. They are best suited for very picky trout: those rising in flat water, where both the fish and the angler can easily see the fly, and those that have refused other patterns while feeding during a hatch in slow-moving water.

Hackle Stacker Style

Bob Quigley's Hackle Stackers are tied similarly to parachute-style flies, and they're used to imitate mayfly emergers, duns, and spinners. Their tails are usually made from divided Microfibetts or hackle fibers. But they can also be tied with trailing shucks. Bodies are usually made from dubbing or stripped quills. The hackle for this style is wound around a post (often made from monofilament), just like a parachute, but the post is pulled forward and tied down behind the hook eye. This forces the hackle to sit in a clump on top of the body, forming wing and leg impressions while also providing floatation. Hackle Stacker flies float flush on the surface and can be difficult to see in riffled water. They are best used for trout rising in slower pools and braided water and for imitating spent insects or those mayflies that emerge in the surface film.

Doug Swisher and Carl Richards invented the No-hackle style and promoted it in their book *Selective Trout*. It's very effective for picky fish in slow pools, but the fly floats poorly and can be somewhat brittle, as the wings can shred easily. Some tiers use synthetic materials instead of the goose feather pictured here to increase the fly's durability. The Hackle Stacker style, created by Bob Quigley, is a very durable, flush-floating fly that uses chicken hackle to imitate a mayfly's wings and legs at the same time. But this fly can be tricky for new tiers to tie well.

Inverted Style

Inverted-style dry flies, or those tied with their hook point intended to ride upside down, above the water rather than below it, are somewhat controversial. I think of this style as one of dry-fly tying's Holy Grails—always just out of reach from being perfected. Many flies have tried: the USD Dun and Roy Christie's EasyPeasy USD Dun, Waterwisp flies, and others. The desire to create a dry fly that floats with its hook point out of the water is born from the belief that if trout can sometimes be selective to very small changes in dry-fly construction, then how are they not bothered by that metal hook in the water?

Many years ago, I became obsessed with perfecting an inverted-style dry fly, and I spent a great deal of time experimenting with them. This culminated in a series of flies I called Flip Flop flies, which I featured in a magazine

Extended-body-style dries can be tied in varying ways with various materials. The one trait they have in common is that the body extends from the hook shank, like this Sulphur pattern tied by Charlie Meck. Inverted-style dry flies, those riding upside down, are probably the least likely dry-fly style you'll find in your local shop. But Water Wisp flies and USD Duns are very popular with some anglers. And you may find others, like this Flip Flop designed and tied by the author.

article for the *Mid Atlantic Fly Fishing Guide*. Flip Flop flies were tied on fine-wire scud or swimming nymph hooks, and they would land hook point up most of the time. But sometimes they didn't, hence the name Flip Flop, because I couldn't be sure how they would land. The fish didn't seem to care, and the flies worked most of the time.

I have largely moved on from this style for several reasons. Inverted flies can make it difficult to hook fish because these patterns usually have materials to imitate the wing in front of the point. The weight of the hook's bend and the materials used to imitate wings want to make the fly turn over and ride like a traditional fly much of the time. And let's face it, the vast majority of dry flies have their hooks in the water and trout still eat them, right? So maybe it's not that important after all. But I still do carry a few inverted flies, and they'll occasionally catch a fish that has refused more traditional offerings. Most inverted flies are not particularly buoyant and are best fished to imitate mayfly duns or cripples for ultraselective trout rising in flat pools.

Extended-Body Style

Extended-body flies have wings, tails, and hackles designed like all the other dry-fly styles I've discussed. The key to this style is that their bodies extend from the hook shank. They can either extend partially, jutting out from the hook bend, or the whole body may be attached only at the end nearest the hook eye, allowing it to move freely from the shank. Extended bodies are most often made from foam, synthetic yarn, deer hair, or even porcupine quills. One of the style's benefits is that smaller hooks can be used in their construction because the entire length of the shank isn't needed to form the body. This can aid their floatation, without the weight of a larger hook. But the flies are sometimes brittle due to the way their bodies are attached, and they are more easily broken or torn from the hook. I also believe that it is more difficult to hook fish with extended-body flies because the body's extension can be inadvertently bumped by a trout's lip as it attempts to eat it, pushing the fly away from its mouth. Most extended-body flies are used to imitate large mayfly duns or spinners in flat pools.

Emerger and Cripple Style

Emergers and cripples form some of the most effective dry-fly patterns because they emulate one of the most vulnerable mayfly life cycle phases.

Emerger- and cripple-style dry flies are found in every fly shop in the country. They have become very popular for catching difficult trout that will not eat other dry-fly patterns. The one trait these flies have in common is that they lie differently in the water from all other standard dry flies. Emergers like the CDC Burke Emerger and the deer hair-wing March Brown Emerger (pictured here) hang on the surface by their wing while the rest of the fly is submerged. Other flies like Renee Harrop's Last Chance Cripple use a parachute hackle to suspend in the water.

These flies usually have one important trait in common: most of the fly is designed to ride below the surface while only a small portion of it, generally a buoyant wing made from feathers, hair, or synthetic materials, is visible above the water. This makes it important to add floatant only to whatever part is supposed to float—you want most of the fly to sink. That way it looks like a mayfly just breaking through the surface film or one that is trapped. These flies are best employed in stream areas with slow to moderate current because they are easily submerged due to the fact that most of the fly is already wet. For the same reason, they are also difficult for most anglers to see on the water. Design elements from many of the previously mentioned styles can be used to create the floating portion of an emerger/cripple-style fly.

Down-Wing Style

Down-wing dry flies are most often intended to imitate mayfly spinners after they have released their eggs and fallen spent to the water, though some fly tiers incorporate a brightly colored dubbing ball at the bend of the hook to

Down-wing-style flies (also known as spinners) are intended to imitate mayflies that have completed their life cycle and have fallen spent (dying) to the water. The flies can be found with varying body materials, tails, and wings like the CDC, hackle, and poly-wing flies pictured here. But they are all tied with wings outstretched from the body.

Anglers will find other dry-fly types in their local shops that are different from the most commonly found fly styles I've included in this book. But you can look at the components of those flies and get a good idea of how you're supposed to use them. For instance, the parachute hackle tied on the underside of this Truform Emerger, designed and tied by the author, tells you that these flies are best suited for flat-water applications like pools—similar to the parachute-style flies discussed previously.

imitate spinners still carrying their eggs. Trout can occasionally key in on this. The flies can also be used to imitate duns that have been blown over and trapped in the film during windy days. Down-wing flies can have tails made from a single clump of material, often hackle fibers, or divided tails made from hackle barbs or Microfibetts. Bodies are usually dubbed or made from hackle quills. The defining characteristic of this style is its two wings, one tied to each of the fly's sides at 90-degree angles to the hook shank. The wings are often made from synthetic yarns designed to provide the pattern with floatation, but hackle fibers, CDC feathers, and even deer hair clumps are also commonly used. These flies are not very buoyant and can be difficult to see on the water because they ride flush on the surface. They are best suited for fish sipping flies in flat pools.

Other Styles

The 10 mayfly dry fly styles I just outlined will give you a foundational understanding of the most commonly found patterns in your local fly shop's bins. But this list will not cover all of the flies you may encounter, and this will be the same for the caddis, stonefly, and attractor fly styles in the next chapter. One of fly fishing's few constants is our love for developing and naming new fly patterns. Every season, commercial fly-tying companies begin their catalogs with a list of the new designs. And this will never end. It's part of what makes the sport so much fun. You can find Truform flies, Loop-Wings, Cracklebacks, and a whole host of other flies that I've not discussed in this section in some shops and not in others. Sometimes you'll find a dry fly that was invented by the shop owner and it exists only in his or her shop. But when you encounter a dry-fly style that you've not seen before, compare it to the most common fly styles that I've discussed. Look to see similar design elements from one style to the next, and you'll be able to determine how the inventor intended the fly to be used. And then try it.

3

Flies for Other Aquatic Insects and Terrestrials

CRUCIAL POINTS
- Imitating caddisflies, stoneflies, midges, and other aquatic insects with dry flies can be just as important as imitating mayflies on any given day.
- Terrestrial, or land-based, insects are vital for dry-fly fishing during the summer months.
- Understanding fly pattern style characteristics is critical to imitating these other insects.

While it's the beautiful mayflies that get the bulk of angler attention, on any given day a whole host of other insects can inspire trout to rise. Understanding these bugs and showing them the same respect as mayflies in your fly pattern selection can often be the difference between catching trout and leaving the stream defeated.

THE CADDIS LIFE CYCLE

Caddisflies begin their lives as eggs, deposited into the water by females, just like mayflies. Their eggs hatch into caddis larva, which look like little worms and live subsurface like mayfly nymphs. The larvae usually build some sort of structure from bits of plant material, sand, or their own spun silk. Some of them crawl around with their homes on their backs, similar to hermit crabs. Other species build nets like spiders to catch their food, and some freely wander around like many mayfly and stonefly nymphs, without a home structure. Caddisflies in the egg and larva stage are of no importance to dry-fly fishermen.

Each year, around the same time of year and always in the same species-specific order, caddis close their cases or spin their silk into a cocoon and enter a resting stage known as pupation. Unlike mayflies, caddis are considered to

A Green Caddis (*Rhyacophila* sp.) larva. Caddis larvae live on the stream bottom, and though they are very important to nymph fisherman, they don't interest dry-fly fishers until they transform into pupae, adults, and egg layers.

Green Caddis pupate underwater, inside cocoons they make from their own silk. Other caddis species use rocks or bits of plants and sandy detritus to protect themselves during pupation. Caddis pupae are unimportant for dry-fly fishing until they break out of their cocoons and move toward the surface to take their first flight. They are then actively pursued by trout, but often eaten just beneath the water's surface.

This Green Caddis adult looks similar in form to nearly every other caddis adult. But various caddis species will be different in size, color, and markings. Non–fly fishers sometimes confuse caddisfly adults for moths.

have a complete life cycle because of this extra development stage. It's during pupation that caddis transform from water-living worms into air-breathing, winged adults that look similar to moths. Once pupation is complete, caddis chew through their cases and ascend to the water's surface to complete their life cycle. And now they become important for dry-fly fishing.

Most anglers imitate emerging caddis pupae with sunken nymph patterns and wet flies. But this is also a good time for dry-fly anglers to fish "damp" dry flies when fish appear to be eating near the surface. Once caddis adults break through the surface film, they usually flutter and flop as they attempt to take their first flight. This commotion often inspires trout to surface feed, sometimes with splashy, explosive rise as they attempt to eat these moving targets. Anglers will sometimes intentionally twitch and skitter dry-fly patterns across the water's surface to imitate this movement.

Caddis males and females gather over riffles to mate and complete their cycle. The females lay their eggs in the water just like mayfly spinners, with some dipping or dropping them while still in flight and others landing beside the water and crawling to the stream bottom. Once their eggs have been deposited, females float helplessly toward, or on, the surface, just like spent mayfly spinners. Anglers call these dying insects spent caddis.

Spent caddis often present the best dry-fly opportunities. They are easy meals as they float and twitch helplessly in the water, unable to escape the feeding trout. Most dry-fly patterns should be fished drag-free to imitate these trapped insects.

COMMON CADDIS DRY-FLY STYLES

Elk Hair Caddis Style

The Elk Hair Caddis, invented by Al Troth, is by far the most common caddis dry fly used today. The style comprises a dubbed body with a palmered hackle and a splayed deer hair wing. This style can be used to imitate any type of caddis by changing hook size and the color of the materials used to tie it. Elk Hair Caddis float very well because of their buoyant wings and because their palmered hackle keeps their bodies from contacting the water. This makes them an excellent choice for fishing riffles. Elk Hair Caddis are particularly effective for skittering—making the flies intentionally drag and move across the water's surface to make them look alive.

X-Caddis Style

If you take an Elk Hair Caddis, remove the palmered hackle, and add a trailing shuck, you get an X-Caddis. The X-Caddis, invented by Craig Mathews, sits flusher on the water's surface and is most often used to imitate emerging caddis. But if you remove the shuck with your nippers streamside, you can

The Elk Hair Caddis, invented by Al Troth, is the most commonly found caddis dry fly in the world. It's easy to tie, it floats terrifically, and the fish love it, especially in riffled water. But the X-Caddis style, developed by Craig Mathews, is often a better choice for fish eating caddis in flat or slow-moving water. The lack of hackle on the body makes the fly sit flush on the surface.

very easily turn an X-Caddis into a spent caddis imitation. X-Caddis are less buoyant than Elk Hair Caddis because they lose the added floatation provided by the hackle and because their dubbed bodies are in contact with the water. They still float well enough to be used in riffles, though their flush-sitting profile makes them an excellent choice for fishing caddis hatches in slow pools and braids.

Parachute Caddis Style

Parachute caddis are most commonly tied with a dubbed or peacock herl body, a buoyant wing often made from deer or elk hair, and a parachute hackle wrapped around a post. Because these flies are aided in their floatation by two style elements—a hair wing and a parachute hackle—they float very well and are an excellent choice for fishing heavy riffles and pocket water. These extra style elements make the flies bulkier, and they are generally less effective in slower-water applications. Some patterns substitute feather wings instead of hair wings, making the flies less buoyant but more sparse-looking for flat-water applications.

Foam Caddis Style

Foam caddis trade realism and subtlety for increased floatation. They are constructed either by wrapping closed-cell foam around a hook shank to form a body or by using foam to make their wing. Foam floats better and longer than deer hair, but it's more difficult to fashion into a lifelike form. These flies tend to be less durable than Elk Hair or X-Caddis, but they are great searching flies for blind casting in riffles and pools or for use in fly tandems. You won't have to dry and dress (add floatant to) the flies as often to keep them floating, and they can be tied to match most caddis hatches. But anglers are limited by the color options available in foam.

CDC Caddis Style

Anglers will usually find several CDC caddis variations at their local fly shops. Some patterns are composed entirely from CDC feathers. These flies are made by wrapping CDC around the hook shank to form a body, and then

Parachute caddis add a little more floatation, due to their parachute hackle, than the X-Caddis. It makes them a good, subtle choice when the fish are rising in fast water but not eating an Elk Hair Caddis. Foam caddis style can be tied similarly to any of the other caddis styles. It's the use of synthetic foam, either as a body, wing, or both, that connects these flies. The foam helps the flies float longer than those using natural materials like fur and hair. But foam looks a little less "buggy" and sometimes gets refused by the fish because of it.

CDC-style flies can either use CDC feathers to build the entire fly—body, legs, and wing—or they can be tied like Hans Weilenmann's CDC and Elk, which uses the feathers to form only the fly's body and legs. Feather-wing caddis-style flies have been around a long time. They excel in flat-water applications but also offer enough floatability for use in riffles. The Henryville Special pictured here, invented many years ago by Hiram Brobst in Pennsylvania, is probably the best-known example and still common in fly shops today.

overlaying CDC feathers to form wings. The flies are sparse in appearance, and they're great for use in flat pools. Other CDC caddis are tied with dubbed bodies, using CDC feathers only as a wing. But perhaps the most popular CDC caddis style is really a crossover between a pure CDC caddis and an Elk Hair Caddis: the Hans Weilenmann CDC and Elk. This fly uses CDC as an underwing, tied beneath a standard elk hair wing. The CDC aids floatation and provides a very buggy appearance. These buoyant flies work very well in fast-moving, riffled water and in flatter pools.

Hair- or Feather-Wing Caddis Style

Hair- or feather-wing caddis, just as their names imply, use feathers or a clump of hair (not usually flared like an Elk Hair or X-Caddis) tied and swept back over their bodies to imitate caddis wings. This fly style doesn't float as well as others, so tiers usually incorporate hackle, either palmered over their bodies like an Elk Hair Caddis or, most often, tightly wound at their heads like a standard-style mayfly pattern, to help them float. The Henryville Special is probably the most commonly found feather wing–style caddis, but there are many others. Hair-wing caddis look very similar, except wing feathers are replaced with a clump of hair. A pattern like the Chuck Caddis uses woodchuck guard hairs for its wing. Both hair- and feather-wing caddis are most often used in calmer water because of their slimmer, less bulky profiles reduce their buoyancy. They can be used in moderate riffles as long as the angler is willing to dry and redress the flies more often.

Deer Hair Body Caddis Style

The most obvious characteristic of this caddis style is the use of spun and clipped deer hair to create caddis bodies and wings. You spin deer hair by taking a clump of it and wrapping it loosely around the hook shank with thread before pulling the thread tight to make the hair flare. This is done with

Extended-body caddis styles, like this Slickwater Caddis, can be tied many different ways. Just like extended-body mayfly-style flies, their defining characteristic is having a body that is detached from the hook. Deer hair body flies are usually made by spinning deer hair on the hook and then trimming it into shape, like this Goddard Caddis designed by John Goddard and Clive Henry. The hollow hair makes the flies very buoyant.

several clumps, depending on the size of the fly. The hair is then trimmed into shape to imitate just the caddis's body in an Irresistible Caddis, or to imitate both the body and wing in a Goddard Caddis. Most deer hair body–style caddis also incorporate hackle in their construction to imitate legs and aid floatation. This caddis style floats very well and is an excellent choice for fishing rough water.

Extended-Body Caddis Style

Extended-body caddis styles, just like similar patterns already discussed for mayflies, allow anglers to tie larger flies on smaller hooks, helping the patterns weigh less and aiding floatation. Their extended bodies are often created with synthetic yarns or chenille, and many of these flies have a sparse appearance that makes them an excellent choice for flat-water applications. Their optimal use is ultimately determined by the other characteristics used in their construction, such as a standard or parachute hackle or the incorporation of foam materials. But what these flies gain in a more realistic form, I believe they sometimes lose in fish-hooking ability, as trout can bump the extension with their mouths, sometimes causing failed hook sets. I find this hooking problem less common with extended-body caddis than with mayflies because the caddis extensions are generally much shorter to imitate the smaller caddis bodies. But it's still something to consider if you're missing fish with an extended-body caddis-style fly.

Egg-Laying Caddis Style

A brightly colored ball, often made from dubbing tied at the bend of the hook to imitate a caddis's egg sac, is the common trait for this caddis dry-fly style. These flies can be important during the caddis egg-laying life cycle stage, as the fish seem to key in on the extra nutrients the egg sac provides. Nearly all caddisfly styles, except extended-body caddis, can be easily transformed into egg-laying style by adding an egg sac. The flies tend to be most effective when fished in the riffle areas where caddis deposit their eggs.

Synthetic Caddis Style

The vast number of synthetic fibers available to today's fly tiers has created a whole category of synthetic-winged and -bodied caddis imitations, and you'll see several variations at most fly shops. Synthetic materials provide a couple of important attributes over natural materials: they generally float very well, they are quite durable, and they offer a disheveled, buggy appearance. The Iris Caddis, Enrico Puglisi's EP Fiber Caddis, and many others excel in both rough and calm water. The first magazine article I published was for my own synthetic caddis–style fly I call the Clearfield Caddis. This pattern, like many others, incorporated natural materials for its body and legs, with a

Synthetic caddis style is defined by the use of synthetic, nonnatural materials to tie the fly. Often, these flies are a mixture of the two material types, like this tan caddis with a precut foam wing and a chicken hackle. But some use only synthetic materials to form the entire fly, making them more buoyant but often less buglike in appearance. Any caddis style can be made into an egg-laying style by simply forming a brightly colored egg sac near the bend of the hook, like this hair-wing style turned into and egg layer.

synthetic trailing shuck made from Flashabou and a wing treated with Water Shed (a commercially available waterproofing agent for fly tying) and made from synthetic yarn.

THE STONEFLY LIFE CYCLE

Stoneflies do not have a resting or pupation stage like caddisflies. Their life cycle is completed more similarly to that of a mayfly. But the manner in which they complete their cycle makes them much less important for dry-fly fishing than most mayflies.

Stoneflies require very clean, well-oxygenated water, though some species are more pollution tolerant than others. They hatch from eggs deposited in riffles and grow as nymphs, beneath the water's surface, for one to three years, depending on the species. At approximately the same time of year, and

Stonefly nymphs (*Pteronarcys* sp. is pictured here) live for up to three years once they hatch from eggs. The physically larger the species, the longer it takes to develop. Stonefly nymphs usually emerge into adulthood by crawling onto dry land, so they are unimportant for dry-fly fishing. But there are some exceptions, like Eastern Early Black Stoneflies (*Taeniopteryx* sp.), which I have witnessed emerging in water and inspiring trout to rise.

There is a period of time after aquatic insects emerge—how long depends on many factors, including air temperature—when the insects pump fluid into their wings, allowing them to unfurl and harden, enabling flight. They are nearly helpless until after this occurs. Trout can key in on insects that do this on the water's surface. But the stonefly pictured here is safe on dry land.

Stonefly adults like this Salmonfly (*Pteronarcys* sp.) can create explosive dry-fly fishing opportunities when they clumsily fly into the water or land there while depositing their eggs, but they spend most of their adult lives climbing around dry land, safe from the trout.

always in the exact species-specific order (just like the other aquatic insects), stoneflies emerge into winged adults. But this emergence, unlike the mayfly and caddisfly emergences, seldom inspires surface-feeding trout.

Most stoneflies crawl outside the water, onto rocks, to emerge, so trout don't have the opportunity to eat them. But in some isolated instances, and with some species more likely to do so than others, stoneflies will emerge in the water. This usually happens with early spring species when the water is high and streamside rocks are submerged. Some mayfly species like *Isonychia*, which prefer to emerge outside the water, on dry ground, can also emerge in-stream if forced to do so by high water.

This in-water emergence is controversial, and some say that it doesn't occur. I once conducted an experiment where I filled an aquarium to its top, so the water was almost spilling out of it. I left no dry areas for insects to emerge outside the water. I then collected stonefly nymphs from a nearby stream, put them in the aquarium, and waited for them to hatch. They eventually did, even though they were prevented from reaching dry areas. I found some of them dead, floating on the surface, apparently drowned. But others were able to escape and fly to safety. For me, this verified what I thought I was seeing in nature and proved that some stoneflies can emerge in water if they are forced to do so.

Once these insects have emerged from the water into winged stonefly adults, they provide the best opportunity for dry-fly fishing. But it's usually by accident. Stoneflies mate on dry ground, like caddisflies, and unlike mayflies, which mate while flying. Stoneflies then usually crawl from dry land to lay their eggs in riffles. But stoneflies are very clumsy fliers, and their unstable flights from streamside vegetation in search of mates often leads to them falling into the water, where they struggle mightily, garnering attention from surface-feeding trout. Trout love these often very large meals, and dead-drifting, twitching, and skittering stonefly dry imitations can trigger explosive rises from the fish.

COMMON STONEFLY DRY-FLY STYLES

Chubby Style
The Chubby Chernobyl, most often just called the Chubby, is one of the most commonly found dry flies in western anglers' boxes, though the fly is becoming more popular in the East as well. The Chubby has a Krystal Flash tail, a dubbed body, a single-layer (most of the time) foam overbody, rubber legs, and wings comprising two clumps of white synthetic yarn. Chubbies are highly buoyant, very visible, and can be purchased in a wide array of colors and sizes. They are not only excellent imitations for stonefly dries, but also work very well for imitating grasshoppers. The flies catch fish in both riffles and pools, and once runoff subsides, I may tie a Chubby to my leader every day of the season for nearly a month. It's one of my best searching patterns in southwestern Montana trout waters.

Stimulator/Sofa Pillow Style
Long before anglers began using synthetic materials and foam to construct stonefly dry-fly imitations, the Stimulator and Sofa Pillow reigned supreme. These two patterns aren't very different from each other, though the original Sofa Pillow called for very specific materials. I consider them a single pattern style, with various materials added or removed to achieve specific effects. Both flies can have either dubbed or floss bodies, or a combination of both. And the bodies can be either a single color or two-toned. Their deer hair wings and tails, combined with palmered hackle tied over their bodies and multiple hackle turns at their head, make them float very well. Stimulators and Sofa Pillows can be tied very small to imitate the tiniest stoneflies or huge for Giant Stones. They work best in riffled water but will also catch fish in slower pools, particularly near streamside vegetation where a clumsy stonefly might inadvertently fly into the water.

Stimulator style, popularized by Randall Kaufmann and Jim Slattery, is very similar to the older Sofa Pillow dry fly created by Pat Barnes. The flies are both heavily hackled and very buoyant for fishing in heavy riffles and braids. The Chubby Chernobyl, more commonly called the Chubby, has become perhaps the most often used stonefly dry imitation. And that's probably because it looks like many different bugs—from a stonefly to a hopper to a cricket. Whatever the fish think it is, they love it. And it's my favorite fly to use in a tandem with a nymph dropper.

Stacked Foam Style

Stacked foam–style dry flies, like the Club Sandwich, Amy's Ant, and many other patterns, take multiple sheets of often different colored foam, tied together, to form their bodies. Most of the flies in this style will have rubber legs and an overwing made from deer hair or a buoyant synthetic material. The flies are often large, very buoyant, and usually gaudy in appearance, which makes them an excellent choice for blind casting during stonefly hatches in riffles, in braided water, and near streamside vegetation. Like many stonefly patterns, they work well as hopper imitations. They are also a very good choice for prospecting with tandem rigs.

Bullet-Head Style

Bullet-head flies use deer or elk hair, tied near the hook eye and pulled back along the body, to give them a very distinct bullet-head shape. They

Stacked foam–style flies incorporate multiple colors of closed-cell foam to create their bodies. There are many flies in this style, being marketed under many different names, that are all slightly different yet maintain the same multiple foam use. Bullet-head style have a hair head that is pulled back over their body to form the fly's head and overwing. The flies are bulky and somewhat air resistant (most of these large stonefly imitations are), which requires anglers to use heavy tippets so the flies do not spin in the air, twisting the leader.

are designed for fishing areas of calmer water or anywhere a more realistic looking stonefly form is required when other, bulkier flies are getting refusals from the fish. Most of the flies also incorporate rubber legs, but not always. Bodies can be dubbed from fur or made from deer hair, foam, or other synthetic materials. Bullet-head dries with extended bodies are often used to imitate the largest stoneflies. Bullet-heads float very well for use in riffles, though their flush-floating profiles can sometimes make them difficult for anglers to see. Their more realistic shape also makes them a great choice for fishing pool edges along the banks.

Trude/Hair-Wing Style

According to Kelly Galloup's Slide Inn website, the Trude-style dry fly was invented by Carter Harrison in the early 1900s. Harrison took an existing wet-fly pattern and altered it to float. A traditional Trude has a tail made from golden pheasant crest feather fibers, a hair wing made from calf tail, and

Trude or hair-wing style is a very old way of tying dry flies; the Trude was designed in the early 1900s by Carter Harrison. Trudes in large sizes are excellent stonefly imitations. But they also work well for caddis if tied smaller. Most stonefly dries can be transformed into parachute style by adding a parachute hackle. Perhaps the best example is Doug Swisher's PMX, which would be a bullet-head style if not for the parachute hackle. The hackle increases the flies buoyancy and gives it a more substantial appearance. Sometimes big fish want big meals.

hackle tied near the hook eye, tied like a standard-style mayfly pattern. But this style can incorporate many different types of feather fibers for the tail and a whole host of furs for the wing and yet retain the general Trude form. Bodies can be made with many materials, from dubbing to foam. Peacock herl is often used. Trudes are most effective when tied to imitate small to midsize flies. They aren't as buoyant as the other stonefly dry styles, so they are best used in pools or less-turbulent riffled areas. Trudes look very similar to hair wing–style caddis patterns, but a Trude will have a tail made from hair or feather fibers. Caddisflies, and their imitations, do not have tails.

Parachute Style
Perhaps the most common parachute-style stonefly imitation is Doug Swisher's PMX, but there are others. The parachute-style stonefly looks very similar to the parachute-style caddis, but the stoneflies are usually tied in larger sizes and often incorporate rubber legs into their construction. These flies,

like many of the stonefly dries, can also be used as hoppers or just general attractor patterns. They are most effective when fished in riffles or areas near streamside vegetation in slow pools.

MIDGES

Common Midge Dry-Fly Styles

Mayflies, caddisflies, and stoneflies often get the greatest amount of angler attention, but there are days, lots of days, when midges are the most important aquatic insects for dry-fly fishing. This is particularly true for cold, relatively temperature-stable streams with reduced insect diversity, like spring creeks and tailwaters or streams recovering from a pollution event in which other types of aquatic insects have been lost. Some midge species are pollution tolerant, and they will often be the first aquatic insects to return to a recovering stream. Late fall, winter, and early spring often provide the best midge fishing, but it's possible to find these diminutive insects, and trout eating them on the surface, most days of the year.

There are entire books dedicated to fishing midges and their imitative fly patterns, and if catching trout on tiny flies tied to tiny tippets is your preferred way to fish dry flies, or you often fish streams where midges are

Midges don't mind cold weather, as these adults lazily sunning themselves on a winter's day ice shelf can attest. But if the water temperature is too cold, it could inhibit the trout's desire to rise, as their metabolism is diminished.

Midge dry-fly styles can be broken down into two types, though there is a lot of variation among these types: those designed to imitate a single midge, and those meant to imitate a group of mating midges. Created by George Griffith, the Griffith's Gnat, to the right of the CDC Midge, is by far the most common midge cluster dry fly.

Midges can sometimes hatch in unbelievable numbers. These tubes are all midge larvae shucks from insects that emerged on a spring day along the Yellowstone River. It's often their sheer volume that inspires trout to rise for such tiny insects.

particularly important, then you may want to have a larger midge dry-fly arsenal than I normally carry. I usually have midge emergers and adult patterns in three primary colors: black, olive, and cream or white. And though it's very possible to find other color midges hatching, I nonetheless can usually convince the trout to eat one of the three shades I'm carrying.

The vast majority of midge dry-fly pattern styles can be grouped similarly to mayflies, with standard, parachute, and CDC Compara-dun probably being the most commonly used to imitate adults. Midge emergers are also tied similarly to mayfly emerger patterns with CDC and parachute versions, like the Sprout, widely available in most fly shops. Trout will sometimes focus upon mating clusters of midges. The Griffith's Gnat, created by George Griffith, was designed to imitate this cluster, and it's the most common mating midge pattern. One of the advantages of fishing a Griffith's Gnat is that because the pattern is designed to imitate a group of midges, you can use a much larger fly than if you were imitating a single midge. Tiers also accomplish this by tying two or three individual midge patterns on a larger dry-fly hook. These bigger flies can occasionally work well, but usually only if the hatch is especially heavy.

OTHER AQUATIC INSECTS

Anglers should be prepared to find trout rising to a whole host of other aquatic insects from time to time, though it's most common in the late spring and summer months. Crane fly, Alder fly, fishfly, dragonfly, damselfly, and patterns for other species can sometimes make the difference between imitating what the fish are eating and going home disappointed. But the importance of these flies varies a great deal from stream to stream. And on some streams, they may not even exist or be important to dry-fly fishing at all. But if you find trout eating something other than the mayflies, caddisflies, stoneflies, and midges that I've discussed, it would be beneficial to collect a sample and consult your local fly shop or one of the hatch books I've included in the Selected Reading section at the end of this book to try to match it.

TERRESTRIALS

Common Terrestrial Dry-Fly Styles

Any dry-fly angler who has fished a single summer knows the importance of imitating terrestrials with dry flies. Terrestrials are land-based insects that do not conduct their life cycle in the water. They must fall, fly, or hop into the water for fish to eat them. Blind casting terrestrial patterns toward streamside vegetation, in the heat of the day when these land-based insects are most active, is perhaps the most effective way to catch trout on the surface during

Terrestrials—land-dwelling insects like this flying ant—become trout food by accident when they fly, fall, or hop onto the water's surface. Aquatic insects always get anglers excited, but sometimes terrestrials provide even better dry-fly fishing.

the dog days of summer. Because of this, there are a lot of terrestrial dry-fly options available at most fly shops.

I divide terrestrials into what I consider to be the five most important families: ants and flying ants, beetles, grasshoppers and crickets, moths and inchworms, and cicadas. But there are other types of terrestrials that can be locally important. I see two distinct categories for imitating these five terrestrial families: natural-material imitations and synthetics.

Natural-material imitations are flies constructed most often from deer hair, hackle, and fur, basically any material that existed in nature before we incorporated foam into tying flies. These older, natural-material terrestrials don't float as well and are often more brittle and more difficult to see on the water than modern foam flies. But that doesn't mean they don't catch fish. In fact, on heavily pressured waters where trout see foam flies day after day, trying one of the older, natural-material patterns may lead to more fish in your net. But in spite of this, foam is the king of modern terrestrial fly designers.

Most western fly shops will have entire cabinets dedicated to the many fly patterns designed to imitate grasshoppers with foam. They are common in eastern fly shops, too, but usually you'll find fewer options there. Every year, new ones arrive on the market, claiming to be improvements on the amazing number we already have. Most of these new flies incorporate only a subtle difference between themselves and a preexisting pattern, but sometimes it's the little differences—something trout aren't accustomed to seeing—that inspire a fish to eat your dry fly. In spite of this, I have found that a hopper's shade of color is often more important than the style in which it's tied.

I generally carry hopper patterns in tan, yellow, green, and pink, though there are more options than that at most shops. If you take any of these patterns and tie them with black materials, you've created a cricket, and I carry some of them, too. But seeing a black fly on the water can be difficult at times, so I usually try to get the fish to eat a more visible hopper pattern before I go to my cricket imitations.

It's the same for ants and beetles. Because these flies are much smaller than the average cricket pattern, they are even more difficult to see on the water. But fly tiers aid visibility by using hi-vis parachute posts or tying the top of

This terrestrial group shot is a compilation of the old and new: the old way of tying terrestrials existed before the development of synthetic materials. It's shown here with a Shenk's Cricket, a Parachute Fur Ant, and a Hi-Vis Crowe Beetle. The foam flies are a Thunder Thighs Hopper, a Cow Killer Ant, and a Foam Beetle. The new synthetic flies are more durable and float better than the old style. But sometimes the older patterns catch more fish.

Foam hoppers in various colors and sizes are vital patterns for summertime dry-fly fishing in the West, but they work on eastern streams, too. Bill Kosmer fooled this beautiful Yellowstone cutthroat on a hopper during late-summer, low-water conditions on the Lamar River in Yellowstone National Park.

the fly with a brightly colored foam while leaving the underside black, red, or green to mimic the natural's true color.

Cicadas are much more important in some fisheries than others, usually due to the number of cicadas that live along the waterway. In the eastern United States, black-and-orange periodical cicadas, which appear only every 13 or 17 years, provide some of the best dry-fly fishing of any angler's lifetime. But dog-day Cicadas, which are often shades of black and green, are found every year, east and west, and they also can inspire good fishing for prospecting anglers blind casting them beneath trees.

The final family, moths and inchworms, can sometimes provide excellent dry-fly fishing, though their populations are cyclical and some years they may be relatively unimportant on any given fishery. I had two consecutive years of amazing dry-fly action on the Upper Delaware's East Branch after an infestation of forest tent caterpillars appeared along the river. But in the third year they were gone, a population crash, and they were unimportant the following season. There are exceptions. Spruce moths are a yearly staple for many western trout fisheries.

Moths are often imitated by large versions of Elk Hair Caddis, though some foam imitations have become popular recently. Their larvae, caterpillars and worms, often fall from trees, and trout sometimes notice them. Foam or deer hair worm patterns, intended to float on the surface, can produce great dry-fly fishing when this happens.

4

Choosing the Best Fly

CRUCIAL POINTS
- All dry-fly styles were designed for specific purposes; they will excel at some applications and falter at others.
- Trout can still be caught with dry-fly attractor patterns even when there are no insects appearing on the water.
- The ability to read water is vital when blind casting dry flies.

I've been surprised, over the years, by the number of anglers who've brought their dry-fly boxes into the fly shops I owned or managed and asked either me or my staff to identify each fly's name for them. I guess I'm just not sure how this helps these fishermen. You don't really need to know a fly pattern's name to use it.

What you do need to know is the pattern's strengths and weaknesses: how its designer intended it to be used, and how you can repurpose it to fill your need for any given rising fish. Then you'll know if you should tie it to your leader or choose another. Does it matter if the fish eats your mayfly dry imitation, believing it to be a cranefly? Of course not. Think of yourself as an imaginative carpenter, not only using the perfect tool for the job, but sometimes also using whatever it takes to get the job done. If it works, that's all that matters.

It can be overwhelming to new dry-fly anglers (or even more experienced ones) to see the number of dry flies in a fly shop. How is anyone supposed to know how, or when, to use each of them? The easiest way to get a basic understanding of which dry-fly style to use for a given circumstance is to think of them as fitting into one of the pattern style categories I outlined in the previous two chapters, with each style having its own specific strengths and weaknesses. There are no universally accepted dry-fly style categories in which to place every dry fly, so I've isolated what I believe to be the main styles here only as an aid. But understand that others may see these styles a little differently than I do.

Though it's impossible for every single dry fly to fit neatly into one of my categories, the styles I've chosen will fit the vast majority of flies. And this will help you understand the intended purposes for various dry-fly styles—what they do best, and their limitations. Each style has its own strengths and weaknesses, determined from the way it's constructed: the materials used to tie it, the way these materials are used to imitate specific insects, and the way the materials make the fly float and aid visibility for the angler. But this can be tricky; some patterns have more than one style characteristic built into their construction.

For instance, it's common to find deer hair mayfly emergers that have hackle wrapped around their deer hair wing like a parachute style. So how would you know the best way to use this pattern when it fits into both the emerger and the parachute categories? The first thing to consider is the advantages and disadvantages of parachute- and emerger-style flies, which I outline in their respective sections. Then, think about the way in which combining these two styles makes a new fly better. And what are the drawbacks? I think of it like this: the more style elements used to construct a fly, the busier the fly appears

and the less likely it will work well in water where selective trout can get a good look at it, like a slow pool. But these busier flies will probably float better and be more visible to the angler since they incorporate floatation aids found in two styles. They will often be very good options in faster water and riffles.

So, fewer fly components and style characteristics generally equals flatter water and more delicate presentations. More style characteristics in a fly generally equals faster water, low-light conditions, and often a more visible

Understanding the type of water you're fishing and parring that to the strengths of a particular dry-fly style can greatly increase your chances of success. The slow-moving, clear and flat water in this picture makes me want to begin with a flush-riding pattern such as a parachute style.

pattern. But you'll need to look at each pattern individually. Think about its construction design elements and why it was made that way. Then determine if it's the best option for the hatch you're imitating, the time of day you're imitating it, and the type of water in which the fish are rising to it.

READING THE MAYFLY, CADDIS, AND STONEFLY PATTERNS STYLE COMPARISON CHARTS

The following charts are intended to illustrate the strengths and weaknesses of the various pattern styles listed for mayflies, caddisflies, and stoneflies in chapters 2 and 3. The charts are intended to compare one style against the rest, using a 1 to 5 ranking scale. A 1 ranking means the style is not recommended for this application in relation to the alternative styles listed. It does not mean that the style could never work. So if it's the only style type you have in your box for a particular hatch, then try it. A 3 ranking is neutral; the style isn't as effective as some options, but it will work better than others. A 5 ranking means that the style is ideal. I compare each of the styles by judging its effectiveness with 10 different criteria.

Large Flies: The charts consider any mayfly, caddisfly, or stonefly imitated with a hook size 12 and larger to be a large fly. Large flies are more difficult to keep floating because they are heavier and, being more visible, are easier for fish to discern as fakes. Some styles diminish, and some magnify, these traits.

Small Flies: Any of the three fly types tied on hooks size 14 and smaller are small flies. Small flies are more difficult for anglers to see on the water, particularly during low-light periods, but much easier to keep floating than large dries and less likely to be refused as forgeries.

Flat Water: Flat water is any stream area, such as a pool, where the water is relatively calm, though it also considers areas outside the main current, like backeddies adjacent to riffles. Fish often choose to feed in flat water because they expend less energy to do so. But the reduced current gives trout more time to look at a pattern before the water moves it past the area in which they're holding. Spent insects and those riding the surface for extended periods will often be found in flat water. Fish will also move from areas of current into flat water during periods of low light: cloudy days, sunset, sunrise, and after dark.

Riffles and Braids: These are areas with significant current—the riffles at the top of a pool, the quickly moving water just below a riffle before it calms into a pool (braids), and the pocket water found between rocks and boulders. Fish feeding in riffles and braids are often looking for the aquatic insects that emerge in these areas as well as seeking cover to hide. The moving water gives an angler several advantages: broken current makes leaders and tippet less visible; drag-free drifts are less important because the water is already moving the flies; and fish must make a quick, predatory decision to eat swift-moving flies, making them less selective than fish feeding in slow pools.

Daylight Fishing: Dry-fly fishing from sunrise to sunset.

After-Dark Fishing: Dry-fly fishing after the sun sets.

Sipping Rises: Rises where a trout displaces very little water to eat an insect. Often, only a trout's nose will protrude from the water to eat.

The ability to choose the best dry fly from hundreds of options is often the delineation between good and great dry-fly anglers. This rainbow trout wanted a caddis imitation in the middle of a heavy mayfly emergence.

Sometimes the bug will simply disappear as the fish gently sucks it from below the surface. These types of rises are most often encountered when fish are eating slow-moving insects like spinnerfalls or spent egg layers. Cold weather can also sometimes keep insects from leaving the surface quickly and instigate sipping rises, as can heavy hatches where the trout have lots of options for which insect to eat.

Bulging Rises: A bulging rise is created by a water bubble being formed as a fish reaches the surface to feed. This can sometimes be an indication of a fish excitedly feeding on a heavy hatch, or a fish feeding on emergers or drowned insects just beneath the surface. If the fish is actually eating just below the surface, you may occasionally see its dorsal fin or back as it rises. Most high-floating dry flies will fail to catch fish at this time, but emergers with some of the fly floating subsurface can work very well.

Mayfly Dry Style Chart

Style	Large Mayflies	Small Mayflies	Flat Water	Riffles and Braids
CATSKILL	5	3	2	5
THORAX	4	4	4	3
PARACHUTE	5	5	5	3
COMPARA-DUN	3	5	5	3
NO-HACKLE	2	5	5	1
HACKLE STACKER	3	4	5	3
INVERTED	2	4	5	1
EXTENDED BODY	5	2	4	4
EMERGER/CRIPPLE	4	5	5	2
DOWN-WING	4	5	5	1

Caddisfly Dry Style Chart

Style	Large Caddisfly	Small Caddisfly	Flat Water	Riffles and Braids
ELK HAIR CADDIS	5	5	3	5
X-CADDIS	4	5	5	3
PARACHUTE	5	3	3	5
FOAM	5	2	3	5
CDC	3	5	5	2
HAIR OR FEATHER WING	2	5	5	3
DEER HAIR BODY	5	3	3	5
EXTENDED BODY	5	2	4	3
EGG LAYING	5	5	3	5
SYNTHETIC CADDIS	3	5	4	5

Stonefly Dry Style Chart

Style	Large Stonefly	Small Stonefly	Flat Water	Riffles and Braids
CHUBBY	5	3	5	5
STIMULATOR/SOFA PILLOW	4	5	3	5
STACKED FOAM	5	2	4	5
BULLET HEAD	4	4	5	3
TRUDE/HAIR WING	3	5	4	3
PARACHUTE	5	3	4	5

				Mayfly Dry Style Chart	
Daylight Fishing	After-Dark Fishing	Sipping Rises	Bulging Rises	Splashing/ Gulping Rises	Tandem Fly
5	5	2	2	5	5
5	2	3	2	4	3
5	2	5	4	3	4
5	2	5	4	3	2
5	1	5	3	1	1
5	2	4	4	2	2
5	1	5	3	2	1
5	5	3	3	4	3
5	1	5	5	4	1
4	4	5	2	2	1

				Caddisfly Dry Style Chart	
Daylight Fishing	After-Dark Fishing	Sipping Rises	Bulging Rises	Splashing/ Gulping Rises	Tandem Fly
5	4	2	2	5	5
5	2	5	4	3	3
5	5	3	2	5	5
4	5	2	2	5	5
5	1	5	4	3	2
5	1	4	4	2	2
5	5	3	3	5	5
5	3	3	3	3	3
3	5	4	2	4	3
5	3	5	4	3	3

				Stonefly Dry Style Chart	
Daylight Fishing	After-Dark Fishing	Sipping Rises	Bulging Rises	Splashing/ Gulping Rises	Tandem Fly
5	5	1	1	5	5
5	4	1	1	5	5
5	5	1	1	5	5
5	3	3	3	5	4
5	3	3	2	4	3
5	4	3	2	4	5

The way in which a trout rises to eat a fly (often called its riseform) is a strong indicator of the type of insect the fish is eating and where in the water column it's feeding. By observing this, you can gain insight into the type of fly you want to present to the fish.

Splashing/Gulping Rises: This type of rise pushes the greatest amount of water when a fish reaches the surface. It's often an indication that the trout are chasing a fly that's moving—simply emerging from below the water or skittering across the surface. But trout will also splash or gulp when they are actively feeding on very large insects or particularly heavy hatches and spinnerfalls. I call these "happy" fish. Occasionally, fish will feed this way when an insect falls abruptly to the surface in front of them. Stoneflies, with their clumsy flying abilities, will sometimes cause this to happen, as will terrestrial insects that fly, fall, or hop into the water. Many anglers correctly associate this type of rise with smaller fish chasing caddis.

Use as a Tandem Fly: Fishing dry flies in a tandem is one of the most effective ways to catch trout (see chapter 7). An angler fishes a tandem by using two flies at the same time. You can use either two dry flies or a dry fly and a nymph. If you fish a dry and a nymph, the dry fly becomes a de facto strike indicator that can also hook a fish if it gets eaten. But not every dry fly works well in a tandem. You need to have a dry that floats high on the water to stop it from being constantly pulled subsurface by the nymph. And it needs to be visible for the angler. For the purpose of the charts, I'm only considering using the dry flies in tandem with nymphs.

DRY FLIES FOR NON-HATCH PERIODS

Attractor Flies

Attractor dry flies are most often used when an angler is blind casting, not trying to catch a fish they've already seen rise, but rather fishing the water by casting to areas where they expect a fish to be holding. You can turn any aquatic insect–imitating dry fly into an attractor by using it when the species it's meant to emulate isn't already appearing on the water. For instance, if you're blind casting a size 12 Catskill-style March Brown when you haven't seen any of the naturals, you have turned a hatch-matching March Brown dry fly into an attractor pattern. You can do this at any time—before a hatch has started for the year, during the hatch, or after it has ended— though it usually works best during or after the hatch because the fish have already become accustomed to eating that particular insect.

A hatch-matching pattern that imitates a specific insect or group of insects can be used as an attractor pattern if you use it when the naturals are not evident. The cutthroat in this photo ate a Chubby when no stoneflies or hoppers, which the fly loosely imitates, were around.

It's important to choose a dry-fly style that's buoyant and visible when fishing an attractor in high-gradient mountain streams like the one George Daniel is fishing. The riffled water combined with glare can easily make a flush-floating fly difficult to see, causing you to miss the fish that eats it.

A great time to use hatch-imitating dry-fly patterns as attractors is during sparse aquatic insect emergences where there aren't enough naturals to instigate steadily rising fish, but the trout are opportunistically eating them. Eastern *Isonychia* hatches and western March Browns are examples of this type of attractor fishing, though this tactic can be effective for other hatches, too.

Most of the time when an angler is fishing an attractor dry fly, it's a pattern that really doesn't imitate anything found in nature. Rather, it is something that an opportunistic fish might eat just because it looks like food. There are lots of flies that fit this criteria in most fly shops. So how do you know which one to use when you're fishing?

Perhaps the most important attribute of a good attractor dry fly is your ability to see it on the water. It's not as important for you to be able to easily see your fly on every cast when you're casting to a steadily rising fish. You know where you're casting to that fish, and you have a pretty good idea where your fly should be landing by watching your leader fall to the water. This helps you find your fly even if it isn't especially visible. If you can't see your fly after you cast, simply wait for your fly and leader to float past the fish before casting again. But lift your rod tip to set the hook, just in case, if the fish rises when you think your fly is near it. Do this carefully; you don't want to startle the fish and make it stop rising if it ate something other than your fly. Sometimes you'll hook the fish, and sometimes you'll just have to cast again.

It's not always as easy to find your fly when you're working the water by blind casting. You're moving, the water's moving, and you're often looking forward to the next spot in which to cast—that's a lot of things conspiring to make it difficult for you to find your fly. The type of water and the pattern style you're fishing have a huge impact on this. Less visible, flush-floating flies are much easier to see on flat, slow-moving water than they are in churning riffles. A fly that's difficult to see in one stream area might be a great choice in another. Black-colored fly patterns that can be very difficult to see in low-light conditions will often be the most visible option if you're casting into glare on the water.

An attractor fly's durability is almost as important as its visibility. It might be worthwhile to use a fly that's easily destroyed by a trout's teeth if it's the only pattern that the fish will eat. But you don't want to have to stop and swap out your fly after each fish when you're constantly moving while blind casting,. You'll catch more trout if you don't have to replace a worn fly so often. Flies gain or lose durability by the type and quality of the materials used in their construction as well as the ability of the fly tier who made them.

Flies made from hairs and furs are usually more durable than those tied with feathers. The addition of synthetic materials can also improve a fly's durability. But if you're buying your flies, the manufacturer's tying ability will have a big impact on the flies' durability. Some fly shops and websites sell cheap foreign flies to gain a greater profit margin. But not all foreign-tied flies are cheap. There are varying levels of quality from these manufacturers, ranging from excellent—as good as locally tied flies—to junk. If you buy a fly that falls apart after one fish, the shop or website should stand behind their product and replace it free of charge. If they don't, I'd buy my flies elsewhere. But if you catch a bunch of fish on one fly and then it falls apart, you should probably be satisfied and just tie on another. Flies are disposable, and even the best-tied ones will not last forever.

My final piece of advice is to use something a little different if your attractor flies aren't catching fish. There are times when flies stop being effective after recently working well. This often occurs for me when I fish the same stretch of my home water for several consecutive days, or when the water I'm fishing has recently been pounded by a large group of anglers. There are only so many trout willing to rise in any given piece of water, and they can become very picky if they've been caught a few times with similar fly patterns. So, if you've had great success casting a Royal Wulff for a few days and then the fish suddenly won't eat one, it's time to switch patterns. Often, using something completely different is the key to success. Maybe try using a caddis dry as an attractor, or a terrestrial, if the fish are disinterested in the mayfly style attractors you've been using.

COMMON ATTRACTOR DRY-FLY STYLES

The most commonly found attractor-style dry flies can be grouped into categories just like the hatch-matching styles discussed in chapters 2 and 3. Again, these categories won't contain every attractor fly you might encounter, but they'll cover most of them.

Standard Style

Standard-style attractors are tied in the same general form of standard-style (aka Catskill-style) mayfly dry flies, but they aren't an exact imitation of any living insect. Rather than using materials and colors to match a hatch, they use these things to attract a fish to rise. The Adams is perhaps the most commonly used standard-style attractor dry fly pattern in North America. You can probably find an Adams or one of its iterations—Parachute Adams, Adams Wulff, Delaware Adams, etc.—in every fly shop that caters to trout fishermen. Why is the Adams so universally loved? It's only real attribute is that it looks buggy. Its mix of grizzly and brown hackles combined with its gray-shaded body makes it look similar to a lot of insects, but not exactly like any of them. And that's what the best attractors bring to the table: they just look like something trout would want to eat.

There are many dries that meet the standard-style attractor criteria: Charlie Meck's Patriot, the Royal Coachman, the Quack, and many others. My

This standard-style Adams, first designed by Michigan's Leonard Halladay, wasn't intended to imitate a specific insect. But it just looks like a bug that fish want to eat. Charlie Meck's Patriot, the Royal Coachman, and many other standard-style attractors share the same general form but incorporate differing material to achieve a desired effect. Wulff-style flies, created by Lee Wulff, are tied similarly to standard style, but they incorporate animal hair wings and tails, and they are much more heavily hackled, for fishing in rough, turbid water.

clients and I were having a slow day floating the Yellowstone River during the dog days of summer in 2019. But that changed when I found a few experimental standard-style attractors that I had tied a decade earlier. The flies had simple bodies made by wrapping various colors of Krystal Flash and Flashabou onto their hook shanks, ribbed with thread. They didn't look remotely similar to anything on the water. But they looked buggy, and the fish hadn't seen anything exactly like them before. That was enough for the trout, and it turned our day into a success. Standard-style attractors work well in the same water types as standard-style mayflies: their high-floating hackles make them best in riffles and braids, but they'll sometimes work in slower water, too.

Wulff Style

Wulff-style attractors were invented by fly fishing legend Lee Wulff. He wanted a bulkier fly that would be more buoyant and durable than standard-style dry flies, so he added more hackle turns and changed his wing and tailing materials from hackle tips and hackle clumps into hair wings and tails, usually made from deer or calf hair. The flies' bodies are made from dubbing. Wulffs make excellent prospecting flies, especially for fishing heavy riffles and braids or the pocket water between boulders. The first dry fly I usually tie to my leader for fishing after dark is a White Wulff because its high-standing hackles and broad white wings make it possible for me to see it in moon- and starlight. This technique works especially well for fishing flat pools. But during the daytime, your White Wulff will usually fool far fewer trout because its substantial bulk gives the fish a good chance for close inspection and rejection of the forgery.

Humpy Style

The Humpy's uniquely formed wing is its most outstanding feature. Most tiers create the wings after tying a tail made from a clump of deer or moose hair, but there are other ways to tie the fly. The wing is tied extra long, because it will need to remain approximately the length of the hook shank even after it has been pulled forward over the formed body. To achieve this,

The Renegade style, designed by American Taylor Williams, originated around the same time as a very similar pattern, the Fore and Aft, appeared in Europe. These flies do not look like anything found in nature. But the fact that we're still discussing them 100 years after they were developed should tell you that they still catch fish. The Humpy is descended from an old pattern called a Goofus Bug. Humpies look similar to Wulffs but with a deer hair overbody extending from their tails, along their backs, to form divided wings. All that hollow hair makes Humpies float very well.

the deer hair wing material is allowed to extend above and beyond the tail while the dubbed body is formed. The fact that the body is dubbed over the butts of the wing adds bulk and makes the fly more buoyant. Once the body is complete, the wings are pulled forward, over the body, to form a hump that lends the pattern its name. The wing is then divided, hackles are tied in and wound around the shank, and the pattern is complete. Humpies can be tied in any color imaginable, with the most common being yellow, red, and green. A Humpy can give the impression of a large mayfly or even a terrestrial, like a beetle, because of the pattern's hump. The flies are best fished in the same places you'd fish a Wulff. But the Humpy is even more buoyant than a Wulff.

Renegade Style

The Renegade style attractor is a very old pattern designed in the western United States. It's often used interchangeably with a nearly identical-looking attractor called the Fore and Aft. These two fly types don't look exactly like anything found in nature but are probably taken as a terrestrial insect, though they may also be eaten as a mating midge cluster.

Renegades are generally not great options for fishing flat pools, but they have a couple of excellent attributes for catching trout in riffles and braided water. First, they are often tied with a peacock herl body. Iridescent peacock herl just looks like trout food, and fish often eat fly patterns that incorporate it into their construction. These flies also have two hackle collars, one tied at their hook eye and one at the bend of the hook. The double hackles help the flies float very well, making them an excellent choice for blind casting in riffles. Tiers will often use two dissimilar hackle colors, like cream and brown, to tie the flies. This enhances the angler's ability to see the flies on the water's surface during low-light periods or when glare is a problem. When they really want to show the trout a substantial meal, some anglers tie double Renegades (this is common with Humpies, too). These flies are tied on oversize, long-shank hooks that allow for two identical flies to be tied as a single fly. Double attractor flies are best when fished in the heaviest currents, where you need something to quickly grab the fish's attention and other flies would sink much faster.

Usual Style

Fran Betters, an Adirondack Mountains fly-fishing legend, is the man responsible for the Usual. Usual's were originally tied from just one material: snowshoe rabbit's fur. Cream or white snowshoe hair is often used for the wing and tail, while other shades (gray is very popular) are used to create the body. The basic-colored Usual doesn't really imitate a specific aquatic insect, but it can be tied to imitate any mayfly by simply altering its wing and/or body color. The style can also be altered by substituting materials, yet retain its

Adirondack fly-fishing legend Fran Betters designed the Usual with the novel choice of snowshoe rabbit foot hair to form the fly's tail and wing. This kinky hair holds lots of air bubbles and makes the flies sparse in appearance, yet very buoyant. Foam-style attractors, such as this Hippy Stomper, are very popular with today's anglers and it seems like new ones are released from major fly manufactures each season. These flies can appear very different from one another, but their primary use of foam for increased flotation is the criteria that holds the style together.

basic form and function. For instance, you can replace the snowshoe tail and wing with ones made from CDC. Or use another type of dubbing, such as beaver dubbing, to make the body. Usual-style flies are great tools for fishing both slow pools and riffles and for imitating both dun and emerger mayfly stages. You can sometimes find Usuals tied with hackle palmered over their bodies to make them float better in riffles.

Foam Flies

Foam attractors could also just be called the "other" attractor pattern category. Some of these patterns blur the lines between imitating aquatic insects and terrestrials. Patterns like the Hippy Stomper, Holo Humpy, and many others are great searching flies for fishing during daytime hours between hatches. They're also excellent choices to show the fish something different after anglers have been casting specific hatch-matching flies for weeks on end and the fish are beginning to refuse them. There are too many of these attractors to take an in-depth look at each one in this book. But because they're made from foam, often with a brightly colored foam on top, they'll float well and be very visible. Some have rubber legs. Others incorporate design elements found in other fly styles like parachute- or standard-style hackles. If you're considering purchasing or tying some of these flies, think about how design elements impact the usefulness for other dry-fly styles and then decide what you want this foam attractor to provide for your fishing. And choose one that does it best.

READING THE WATER

You won't catch many trout with your attractor patterns, even if you've picked the perfect one, if you don't know how to read trout water. You read the water when you dissect the river or stream in your mind, thinking about where a fish may be found, even though you don't see one. But how do you know exactly where the fish live?

This question is generally much easier to answer with wild trout. If you're fishing a stocked stream, many of the fish are probably still holding wherever the people carrying buckets put them, most often in a pool. Sure, some fish will move to other areas, but there are several great scientific studies that prove that most stocked fish are clueless. They sit there, waiting to be caught or die, because they don't know what else to do. Sometimes they'll be found in weird spots while they try to adapt to living in current.

These fish have been living in a hatchery raceway, being hand-fed, and they're still trying to figure out exactly what to eat. This is particularly true in the early weeks after they've been stocked. But by the end of the season,

This water contains a pool, a riffle, an eddy, and a glide. The angler's ability to read these various water types and understand where trout are living in them is paramount to catching fish when prospecting (blind casting) with dry flies.

a few of these surviving "holdover" stockies will have figured a few things out. They then begin to behave more like wild fish.

Wild trout live by two primary rules: They live in areas where they won't use more calories to feed than they receive from their food. And they seek cover from predators, most of which come from above the water, whether it's a great blue heron or an angler with a fly rod. But it's important to realize that fish will not hold in the same water all the time. If stream levels drop, one area that provided excellent cover earlier in the year may be void of trout in midsummer. I know a great riffle in Yellowstone National Park's Slough Creek where I catch lots of big fish early in the year, and there's none to be found later in the season. It's the same when water levels rise: areas where the current was once placid at a lower level may not hold fish during high water.

Wild trout will also move within the same section of stream if there's food present. It's very common for trout to move out of a pool and into the riffle at the pool's head if insects are beginning to emerge there. Trout will also drop into very shallow water in the tail of a pool during low-light conditions before dark, throughout the night, and just after sunrise the following morning. Overhead predators can't see them as well without the sun to make them stand out, and they only have to tip their heads a few inches to pluck an insect from the surface.

You want to look for converging cover to find trout when you're reading the water. Fish may not surface feed in a heavy, swift-moving riffle without structure, but add a boulder to break the current, and you've created an excellent pocket in which to cast your fly. Fish also love edges where shallow water begins to deepen. Look for a color change in the stream bottom to find these ledges—the deeper water will be darker—and put your fly right on the edge between the two. A depression in the streambed will also appear darker and may be just deep enough for a trout to lie without fighting the current. This is another area where you should cast.

Areas along a pool where the bank recesses a little can provide a current break to hold a trout. Other spots along a pool where overhanging streamside vegetation provides cover and shade are also places to expect to find fish. Trout often like to lie in one spot and have the food delivered to them by the current. This makes riffles, as long as they're deep enough to cover the fish, a great place to blind cast. But don't neglect the braided water just below a riffle where the current diminishes before it slows into a pool. I've caught some of my largest trout from these areas. It seems daunting at first, but the more you fish with attractor dry flies, the more easily you'll discern where to cast them because you'll have caught fish from similar areas in the past.

5

Pace and Posture

CRUCIAL POINTS
- Your dry-fly fishing goals should dictate your pace.
- Gridding trout water will help you thoroughly cover the water with your flies.
- Your posture and position will either help or hurt your ability to catch trout.

The pace at which you fish is one of the least discussed, yet most import-ant, facets of dry-fly fishing. Fishing pace simply means how fast you move between rising fish, how long you spend blind casting a piece of water before moving to another, and how long you continue casting unsuccessfully before changing flies—basically, how long you do anything related to dry-fly fishing before you stop doing it and do something else. All trout water has sections that produce more, or larger, fish than others. The available time you have to spend walking to, and fishing, these sections is determined by your pace. But the lesser water between these prime areas will hold fish, too, and that's where some anglers get stuck.

I became more keenly aware of fishing pace's importance while guiding the Lamar River in Yellowstone National Park. There's a stretch of the Lamar where I can walk downriver to a small cluster of trees and then fish upriver from there until the Lamar takes me back to the road and an easy walk back to my car. This loop generally takes me about three hours to fish. Yet when I take my guiding clients there, they often take twice as long to cover the same amount of water. And they're not fishing it more successfully than I am. So what is the reason for such a disparity in fishing time?

I've found that one of the biggest hindrances for anglers achieving effec-tive pace is a lack of confidence due to limited experiences. This keeps many anglers fishing too slowly. These fishermen believe that receptive fish are always present, and that their luck could change with the very next cast. They also often don't know what else to do, so they keep doing whatever they feel comfortable doing and expect different results. Take, for example, anglers who continue to blind cast the same fly to a promising-looking area instead of moving, even though they're not generating any interest from the fish. Anglers failing to recognize the importance of pace will often spend too much time in an unproductive spot, and that costs them time they could be fishing better water. The confidence bred from experience tells an angler that sometimes when you're not catching fish, it's the fish's fault, not your technique or even your fly pattern. And there's nothing you can do to change that, other than moving to another spot or trying something different.

Your ideal fishing pace should be set daily by clearly defining and understanding your intentions. Pace can be complicated when fishing with a group of anglers, particularly if all the group members' goals do not mesh. Conflicting angler pace is one of the reasons some of my friends do not like to fish together.

You may also need to readjust your pace throughout the day as your goals, or elements beyond your control, change. Most fishermen decide they're going fishing without

any real thought as to what they want to achieve that day. This is a fine approach if you truly have no expectations, and you'll be happy with whatever the day brings: the stereotypical response is, "It was just good to be out there. The fish are just a bonus." But if you want to catch only big fish, a lot of fish, difficult fish, or any other specific type of fish, then you need to consider your pace.

Generating proper pace is just as important for utilizing marginal water as it is for the best water on any stream. A couple of decades ago, I was fishing a small stream in the Pennsylvania mountains with my friend, Charlie Meck.

The pace at which you fish, whether targeting a rising trout or prospecting with attractor dry flies, will often be the most important factor for your success. Move too fast and you may miss something. Move too slow and you may not catch all that you could have caught. There is a time and place for both. This angler needs to move slowly, or she may be spotted by the fish rising along the bank.

The stream was one I fished often, but it was the first time Charlie and I had fished it together. We worked our way up the creek, catching trout in most of the likely spots. Eventually we reached a very slow, deep pool that held a large dead tree in its center. This pool looked perfect to me at the time, and yet I had never caught a trout from its depths while blind casting

Craig Boslough and I were fishing a Montana spring creek when Craig found a pod of fish gently dimpling the surface as they ate midges. He had to slow his pace, inching his way toward the surface-feeding fish in a slow pool, in order not to push wakes downstream that might have caused the fish to stop feeding.

Craig's proper use of pace allowed him to fool a beautiful rainbow that other anglers might have failed to spot or scared with their approach.

a dry fly. I remember being excited to show it to Charlie because surely this hatch-matching master would unlock its secrets. Charlie and I stood on the pool's edge and I asked him, "So, how would you fish this with a dry fly?" "I wouldn't," Charlie replied. "Or at least I wouldn't spend a lot of time here."

I was initially shocked by Charlie's thoughts. But over time I was able to fully understand what he was saying: Charlie liked to catch a lot of trout when he fished. He knew that this spot, with its nearly nonmoving water that made his dry fly appear lifeless and gave the fish all the time in the world to scrutinize it, would be very difficult. The dead tree's branches, that covered the water would surely catch his leader and flies, tangling and breaking them, forcing him to spend time retying. The chances for catching trout, even just one, wouldn't be great, so why spend time here? Charlie had predetermined his goals for the day and set his pace accordingly. Charlie would make a cast or two around the edges of this spot and move on. There would be easier places, with easier fish, upstream; he just needed to keep moving to reach them.

Recognizing your goals is paramount. Another angler, on another day, may decide that catching a lot of fish isn't very important. Perhaps catching just one from this difficult pool is that angler's goal. For them, spending as much time in this spot to catch that one trout is worthwhile. And that's the fundamental insight for fishing pace: your goals should always dictate your pace. The other important factor is understanding and reacting to the elements beyond your control: weather, time of day, and competition from other anglers.

Weather and time of day often go hand in hand for determining pace. Weather's effect on pace can be as simple as recognizing an approaching thunderstorm and ignoring marginal water to quickly reach the best spots before the deluge falls. Or it can mean slowing your pace on an especially cold morning to work the water more thoroughly for lethargic trout.

Time of day is important, too. Have you thought about how long the fish may be active in the morning before the summer's heat puts them down for the afternoon? Do you want to spend a great deal of time trying to catch one trout in a difficult spot if you know rising stream temperatures will slow the fishing down soon? Maybe. Maybe not. How about the amount

You may have to ignore smaller rising fish and keep moving to cover lots of water to find a large rising brown trout like this. But for some dry-fly anglers, quality surpasses quantity.

of time remaining before the sun sets for the day and you quit fishing because you can't see? What about the time of day a hatch or spinnerfall usually occurs? These things should all impact where you are streamside at a specific time according to your goals, and you need to set your pace accordingly.

PACE DURING A HATCH VS. NON-HATCH PERIODS

Another key factor to determining your ideal fishing pace is whether you're fishing during a hatch. I tend to fish much more quickly during non-hatch periods when I'm blind casting attractor dry flies. The reason for my increased pace is pretty simple: I'm not exactly sure where every fish in the stream that will eat my dry fly is located, so I need to cover as much water as possible to find them. If I fish slowly, I'll cover less water and likely catch fewer fish.

It's different during a hatch. You can see rising fish and know exactly where they are. The only pace question then becomes, "What kind of dry-fly experience do I want today?" If you simply want to catch any fish or as many fish as possible, start casting to the closest fish. Catch it and move to the next. It's important to note that I said "catch it" before you move on.

During intense hatches or during any hatch where a lot of fish are rising, you need to be wary of taking a shotgun approach to the fish. When you shoot a rifle, you have one bullet that will strike the target in one place. With a shotgun, the bullets scatter as they spray at a target. It's the same as dry-fly fishing. You want to choose one target, a single rising fish, and target your single bullet, the dry fly tied to your leader, at a specific spot to catch it. Anglers who shotgun by casting their fly haphazardly into pockets of rising

Some dedicated dry-fly anglers target only rising trout, and they often just watch the water when there are no hatches occurring or fish rising. It's not a bad way to spend the afternoon if you're not itching to catch a fish. Otherwise, it might be time to tie on some nymphs.

fish, or to one fish on one cast, then a different fish on the next cast, tend to catch fewer fish. The reasons are simple.

It's very difficult to figure out what a single trout is taking from the surface if you aren't watching it intently. And you won't be doing that if you're watching several different rising trout at the same time. Steadily rising trout also tend to get into a rhythm when they surface feed, eating insects at identifiable intervals. It can be very important for your fly to reach a rising fish at the appropriate time in this cycle, particularly if the hatch or spinnerfall is heavy and the fish isn't moving from its feeding lane to eat. If your fly floats to the fish just as it has risen to eat a natural insect, the fish probably won't eat your fly on that drift.

Competition from other anglers can have a tremendous impact on pace in our most popular trout waters. Maybe there's a specific pool where you expect the fish to be rising and you've been dreaming about fishing it since your last trip. If you fish crowded water, you may need to completely ignore other water, even if it has rising fish, to move quickly from your car to your dream pool, so you don't find your spot filled with other fishermen by the time you get there. Just realize that it's usually foolhardy to leave rising fish to find rising fish. So maybe you'll take a more relaxed approach and just plan to fish it after the other anglers leave, hoping the fish there are still active. The constant with all of these factors is being a more thoughtful, intentional fisherman, understanding your goals, and adjusting your pace accordingly during both hatch and non-hatch periods. But to be thoughtful, you must be keenly aware of all of the things happening around you. You must be an observant dry-fly fisherman.

BEING OBSERVANT

You have to be observant to the changing conditions around you if you're going to maximize your fishing time. Being observant is perhaps the greatest skill a dry-fly fisherman can hone. A trout stream is always changing. Fish move from one place to the next to take advantage of food sources or due to changing water levels. I try to never tie a fly to my leader until I've spent a few moments looking at the water, scanning for rising fish and observing any insects I might find. And if my rod is already strung from yesterday's fishing, I still take the time to see what's happening today before immediately assuming that yesterday's tactics will work. Even after you begin fishing, your mind needs to be fully engaged and ready to change tactics.

Impatient anglers often charge right into a trout stream, seemingly believing that all the fish are on the far side of the river. Take time to study the water you're about to step into. Or, even better, don't step into the water at all. Cast from the bank. A lot of my guide clients immediately try to march into the water without taking the time to make a few casts with their dry just to see if there's anything there. It's too late once you walk through the water; the fish are scared now.

If you're blind casting dries, think about the type of water where you caught a fish previously or where one refused your fly. Some days, fish feeding patterns evolve, and you'll want to target one type of water over another. For

I nearly missed setting the hook on this beautiful brown trout after a slow day fishing dries. I was glancing upstream when the fish took, hooking itself. Sometimes you get lucky. But it's better to remain observant. (Photo by Matt Grobe)

example, if you caught more trout from the tails of the previous two pools you fished than in the braided water at their centers, consider focusing more attention to the tail of the third pool you find.

Hatches can appear and then diminish quickly. Sometimes you'll catch several fish, and then suddenly the next rising trout won't eat your flies. Something changed. Has a new hatch appeared? Perhaps a different stage of the current hatch is now occurring simultaneously—for example, maybe some mayfly spinners are falling to the water at the same time duns are still hatching. You might not notice these small changes unless you briefly stop fishing and take time to study what's happening around you.

Be thoughtful as to why you're tying one fly to your leader rather than another. In chapter 4 I included charts showing the strengths and weaknesses of the most common dry-fly styles. Consider these fly styles and how they relate to the insects or the type of water you find. Do this before you just grab the first dry fly from your box and start casting it.

One of the reasons so many anglers find fly fishing to be therapeutic is that it takes your mind away from life's troubles and focuses it on something else. If you find yourself thinking about work in the middle of a day's dry-fly fishing, then you're not trying hard enough to catch the trout. Refocus on what's happening in front of you, and you'll be a better angler because of it—and you might just enjoy your day a little more, too.

THE GRID METHOD

The easiest way I've found for demonstrating pace to my guide clients, when blind casting dry flies during non-hatch periods, is by using an imaginary grid to help dictate the number and direction of their casts. I generally instruct these anglers to consider their approach to the water in a 3-square-foot block or grid. The grid begins along the bank on which they're standing and goes upstream for 3 feet. It then extends away from them, toward the river or stream's center, for 3 feet. From there, the grid's outer edge goes downstream, toward them, for 3 feet. The square closes by extending back to the bank on which they're standing.

Each time I work a grid at normal pace (I'll discuss changes to pace speed later), I cast three times as I work my way upstream. The first cast is to the grid's upstream edge, along the bank on which I'm standing. I look for a drop-off, or a division between the often very shallow water along the shore and deeper water toward the center, and use that for my edge. I cast to the top of the grid and strip in slack line as necessary while the fly floats for 3

You should cast your fly on the far side of the grid only after you've fished the water closest to you. If you do it in the opposite order, far side first, you may scare the fish more easily reached with a shorter cast.

feet back to me. Mending is often unimportant because I'm casting on a relatively straight line upstream. Once my fly floats down to me, the bottom end of the grid, I cast again, but this time to the grid's imaginary center line between the inner and outer edges. Once that drift is finished, I end the grid

Water temperature is the driving force for a trout's metabolism. If you're cold while you're fishing, the trout might feel that way, too. It's probably time to slow down. A slower pace worked for John Campbell with this spring creek rainbow on a chilly dry-fly day.

by making one cast to the grid's outer line, the farthest from me. I then take a step or two upstream and begin the grid again.

You'll cover most of the likely trout-holding water when fishing with a grid system. Sure, trout can sometimes be complacent in their feeding and refuse to move a few inches to feed. But this is usually during heavy hatches, when they can afford to wait for the next morsel to come to them. If you just attack the water without a planned approach, you'll often miss some places where your dry should have been cast and spend too much time recasting to places you've already fished, rather than moving to more productive water.

But there are times when more than one cast should be made to each line of the grid; I call this slower grid pace. And there are other times when you should cast only to the grid's center, or along a single edge, and then quickly move on. This is faster grid pace.

Fishing the Grid at a Slower Pace

There are times when fishing the grid with only three casts may not achieve your desired plan for the water, so you'll want to cast more. How much more will be determined by your goals for the day—how far you want to go, whether you want to catch big fish or lots of fish, how eager the trout are in this area—and your own other factors. Here are seven times you should generally slow down and fish the grid at a relaxed pace:

1. Any time the water is especially cold, impeding fish receptiveness. This is usually after a particularly cold night in the spring, fall, or even summer.

2. When you arrive at water where you've caught fish in the past, or water types similar in structure to productive areas you discovered earlier in the day. An important part of being observant when you're blind casting dry flies is noticing the water type where you are receiving interest from the fish. Some days, trout surface feed almost everywhere, and you won't notice a holding trend. Other days, you might find fish more often in one part of the stream like the riffles, braided water below riffles, tops of pools, edges of pools, or tails of pools. You'll want to slow down your pace and concentrate on fishing the grid more thoroughly through these areas.

3. When you reach more obvious trout-holding structures. These places include deeper riffles at the heads of pools, eddies along the bank, scum lines, and any in-stream obstructions like boulders beside deeper water.

4. When a river or stream is overcrowded with anglers, constricting the amount of water available for you to fish. If you've found good water on a crowded day, don't quickly leave it for lesser options.

5. When you've walked or floated as far as you intend to go for that day but want to make sure there isn't one last fish you missed.

6. When a fish has moved to your fly but not eaten it. It's worth trying another cast or two or even changing flies.

7. When you have fish suddenly begin to rise in front of you, and you decide to try to catch them.

Fishing the Grid at a Faster Pace

Just as conditions sometimes dictate prospecting your dry fly through the grid at a slower pace, there will be time when you'll want to fish the grid more quickly. Fishing the grid faster means you'll make just one or two casts for the entire grid and then move on. It can also mean taking more than one or two steps upstream after completing a grid, if the adjacent water is less desirable. Here are seven times you should fish the grid at a faster pace:

1. When the end of the day is approaching and you want to try to catch a few more easy ones before it's over.

Richard Schall decides to quicken his pace before the bison wade into his fishing spot. If you know the water you're fishing is about to be ruined by an outside source—weather, other anglers, wildlife, etc.—cast quickly to the best spots and move on.

2. When the river or stream is crowded with other anglers and there's a particularly good spot you'd like to reach before they get there.

3. During late morning in the summer, as the day and the water are beginning to warm and the fishing is slowing down. You want to strike while the iron's hot.

4. When you haven't been catching fish during a non-hatch period and you're trying different flies and different water types to find a couple fish that will eat.

5. When you have a stream you haven't fished before all to yourself and seeing lots of it is just as important as catching fish.

6. When the water in front of you is marginal—too shallow, too slow.

7. When you don't have the skills to execute the necessary cast in a difficult spot, and you're more interested in catching trout than practicing. Just know that if you never attempt casts beyond your current skill level, you'll never improve. But some days we all really just need to catch some trout.

POSTURE AND GETTING INTO POSITION TO MAKE THE CAST

Posture—how you to stand to cast—is an important element for catching fish. When should you hunch over at your waist, drop to a knee, or maybe even hide behind structure? My answer to all of these: not nearly as often as you might think. Many years ago, I was on a photo shoot with a friend who's also a professional fly-fishing photographer. He told me that I looked "bored and disinterested" in his photos because I stood upright, even though I was catching fish just fine. He asked me to lean behind a rock and intensely cast into the pool above it. I did, and he got his photo.

Fly-fishing books and magazines are full of photos where the angler is crouching or hiding to get advantage on the trout. There are times when this can be important. If you're casting a shadow on the water or trout are fleeing as you approach the stream, then perhaps reducing your stature by kneeling or bending at the waist may help. But don't immediately assume this is necessary. The trout will let you know when you have to take more camouflaged measures—but often, it's for show.

Many of the clients I guide want to crawl around, kneel down, and hunch over along the waters we fish, because they've seen others do it and it looks cool, necessary. But most of the time, anglers can't cast well when they contort themselves in these positions. So instead of potentially scaring the fish by standing too upright, they definitely scare the fish when they make a lousy cast because they're contorted like a yoga instructor. I've found that many of the things we think will scare fish won't, if they are done slowly, incrementally.

I caught this Depuy brown trout by inching toward it. If you look closely, you can see a live Blue-Winged Olive on its back near the wooden net, matching the artificial fly in its mouth.

Montana's DePuy Spring Creek in Paradise Valley has been a great classroom for helping me understand what types of angler movements heavily pressured trout will tolerate. One such lesson came when I noticed a large brown sipping tiny Blue-Winged Olives in a back-spinning (against the current) eddy along the far bank. No matter how I tried, I couldn't get my fly to float drag-free to this fish. I was making longer casts, across the current, because I was worried about spooking it. But this just wouldn't work. The current kept dragging my fly before it had enough time to float upstream to the trout.

So I began creeping closer, from behind the fish, moving only when I could see it rise to eat a natural. Its attention was on its next meal as it rose, and it didn't notice me. Eventually, after moving painfully slow, I was casting just my leader and holding my 10-foot rod above the fish. Now

Kneeling helped my father cast to a trout that was rising at the base of this willow tree. There are times when you have to reposition your body to help you make the ideal cast, but it's usually best to cast from the position in which you're most comfortable.

the fly was able to float unimpeded, and the fish ate it. I've employed this technique of slowly closing the distance between me and a rising trout many times on heavily pressured dry-fly water, from the Upper Delaware River to Pennsylvania's Penns Creek, with great success. But you have to commit to moving slowly. You can't push water and make wakes as you move. I would have spent all day getting into position for that DePuy fish if that's what had to happen.

But you should be aware that what works here won't always work on every stream. Famous trout streams get lots of pressure, and the trout that live there become accustomed to seeing movement from anglers and other creatures like deer and cattle. If they stopped feeding every time a mammal got close to them, they might never eat. On more remote streams, like the legendary sight-fishing waters in New Zealand, fish may not accord anglers so much latitude. But you won't know if you don't try.

I'm not saying that there's never a time to kneel down or try to diminish you physical presence to the trout. Casting to trout rising in clear, slow-moving water during periods of bright sunshine come to mind. But most of the time, if you would simply be more patient, move slowly and cautiously in the water or, better yet, try to stay out of the water, you'll be able to present your dry fly standing as you normally would, without scaring the fish.

You should generally cast to a rising trout from the position where you are most comfortable. For most people, that is usually standing upright with one foot slightly in front of the other, usually the foot that matches your strong hand, though some people operate just fine with their opposite foot forward. The most important part of your stance that I've noticed, from years of guiding anglers, is where you point your hips. The fly almost always goes

Most anglers would be better, more accurate casters if they simply stood and pointed their hips at their intended target. This angler could have been tempted to crouch behind the streamside grasses to obscure himself. But it's much more difficult to cast that way, and it's often unnecessary.

in the direction you point your hips. This is especially true for beginner and intermediate casters. Advanced casters can use their skills to overcome misdirected hips the way the best professional football quarterbacks can break the sacred rule of never throwing the ball across their bodies. But this takes a much higher skill level than most anglers possess.

I've watched many of my guide clients try and try to cast to a rising fish but they can't put the fly where they want to put it, where it needs to go for the trout to eat it. As long as the problem isn't that the cast is too far for them to make (that's almost never the case, because I put them into position where they can reach the fish), the problem is almost always reduced accuracy because they aren't pointing their hips at the target. They have their body slightly twisted and that impacts their accuracy. Once I get them to point their hips where they want the cast to land, they almost always improve.

Once you've identified a rising fish, or water that you'd like to prospect with a dry fly, you need to decide how you're going to approach the spot where the fish is feeding or where you want to cast. One of the biggest problems I encounter when I'm guiding is getting anglers to move their feet to get into the best position. Many people just don't want to walk any more than they deem necessary. But if you cast a shadow at a rising fish because you won't cross the stream to have the sun in your face, you may scare that trout, just because you didn't want to walk.

There are a lot of reasons to move from where you're standing to a better option before casting. Perhaps there is an obstruction in the way of your backcast. Maybe you can achieve a better angle and a longer, drag-free cast if you move. Sometimes the water is moving too fast on the bank on which you're standing, and you can get a better cast to the far bank if you cross.

No matter what your reason for moving, there's one important action you need to take before you do it: put your fly in your hook keeper and reel in your line. Many anglers try to save time by not reeling in their lines while they navigate to the next spot. But, in reality, this is a time and pace killer.

Often, anglers just let their dry fly dangle in the water as they begin to walk. The fly then becomes so waterlogged that it takes a significant effort to get it floating again. Another common maneuver is holding the dry fly with your free hand and letting your leader and fly line dangle as you walk—we've all done this. But this is one of the worst things you can do, as the sagging line invariably catches something and now you've got to spend time untangling the mess you created. Sometimes the line gets caught and the angler doesn't realize it right away, causing the fly to become impaled in the angler's hand.

6

Mending,
Casting Techniques,
and Casting Position

CRUCIAL POINTS
- Controlling dry-fly drag is vital for catching fish.
- Aerial and on-water mends are the key to controlling drag.
- Proper casting position will help you implement mends to control drag.

The perfect dry-fly selection won't help you catch trout if you don't present that fly in a manner in which a trout will receive it. There's a great fly-fishing debate about which is more important: fly pattern selection or fly pattern presentation. Some anglers carry hundreds of dry flies, and they believe that they'll catch more trout because they always have the perfect pattern. Other anglers use far fewer flies—my friend and Catskill fly-fishing legend Ed Van Put is famous for only fishing Adams Parachutes on the Upper Delaware's Main Stem. I tend to believe that both schools of thought are correct, so I generally have lots of flies and try to present them in the best manner possible. We've already examined fly selection. This chapter will help you to utilize those flies.

DRAG
Drag occurs anytime your dry fly moves unnaturally on the water's surface. It's often the primary reason a fish won't eat your fly. I've heard other anglers explain that drag is caused by a fly floating through conflicting water currents that pull it in different directions. But this isn't exactly true. Drag occurs only because your fly is floating through these currents while it is tethered to a stationary object: you.

A turbulent stream such as this, with conflicting currents moving at different speeds and pulling in several directions, will make it impossible to get long, drag-free drifts. Settle for shorter, but more accurate, drifts through likely holding areas when fishing this type of water.

If you drop a dry fly out of your box and onto the water without tying it to your rod, it will float quickly through some currents, spiral over others, maybe even pause nearly motionless in an eddy. It will act just like a living insect, and the fish expect their food to behave this way. If a potential meal doesn't, they'll often quickly deem it a forgery. Would you eat something from your plate that's moving in an unexpected manner? Your fly gets pulled unnaturally only after you lose slack in the system from your rod to the fly. And this is the essence of drag. So to best mimic nature, anglers must purposely resubmit slack into their system, and we do that by mending the line.

Sometimes you'll see anglers cast to a fish and then walk down a bank as their fly floats toward their target. They're trying to extend their drift by moving the tether. My friend Charlie Meck used to call this "walking the dog." But most of the time, anglers must remain stationary as they stand in the water to cast. Creating downstream wakes as you move in the water to prevent drag isn't ideal. Other times, streamside obstructions impede you from walking far enough along the shore for your fly to reach the fish. This is why

to achieve drag-free drifts, under varying conditions, you must be able to mend your leader and fly line to counteract drag from a stationary position.

MENDING

Mending is the way in which anglers manipulate their fly line to help ensure that their dry flies float drag-free to the fish they're targeting. There are two distinct mending categories—aerial mends and on-water mends. In general, aerial mends, which are performed while your fly line is still in the air, are

Arial mends, those conducted before you lay your line on the water, are often the most effective for dry-fly fishing. Mending dry flies on the water, while possible and sometimes necessary, will easily sink your flies if you're not careful.

the most important for dry-fly fishing. If you wait to mend until the fly is already on the water, you'll often cause the fly to sink while trying to mend it, particularly with emerger patterns or other dry flies that aren't very buoyant. You can also pull the fly away from the fish's feeding lane if you mend too aggressively on the water.

Many anglers mend too much. Fly-fishing instructors have placed such a high emphasis on mending that inexperienced anglers believe they have to mend, often multiple times, on every cast. But mending is just a tool to achieve a drag-free drift. So if your fly is already going to float drag-free over the fish you're targeting, there is no reason to mend. And there are several circumstances when you probably shouldn't mend at all.

If you're standing at the bottom of a riffle and casting your fly upstream, toward the top of the riffle, the current will bring the fly back to you drag-free. You shouldn't mend here, though many anglers often do. The only thing you need to worry about in this position is getting too much slack in your fly line as it floats back to you. To counteract this, you need to strip in your fly line as the fly floats downstream. Always keep the fly line between one of your fingers and your rod's cork grip as you strip, or you won't have tension to set the hook if a fish unexpectedly eats your fly. Once the fish eats, simply clamp the line tight between your finger and the cork and lift the rod tip to set the hook. Always make sure to pace your strips as the stream's flow rate dictates. Don't strip so fast that you're pulling the fly or too slow that you're allowing slack to form.

Another time when mending is unnecessary, or even detrimental, is when a fish is feeding in a very tight spot where a long drift isn't possible. Many anglers seem to relish very long drag-free drifts as if that's the whole point of fly fishing. Often, a short, but on-target, drag-free drift is much more effective. Maybe a fish is feeding in a little cut along the stream bank. Or perhaps it's under a bush where your fly will become tangled if it floats too far. In these and other instances, it's best to cast closer to the fish with a shorter drift. Let the fly float without mending, which might sink it or move it away from the fish. Ideally, you want to cast to a fish from a position where you don't need to mend at all but can just let the fly float naturally. That isn't always possible. And that's where good mends can make all the difference between catching a fish or not.

THE MOST IMPORTANT AERIAL MENDS

Reach Cast

The reach cast is arguably the most important mending tool for catching rising fish. If I had to choose between a client with a perfect dry-fly pattern who couldn't execute a reach cast or one with an imperfect fly but a good reach cast, I'd take the better caster every time. The reach cast facilitates the maximum drag-free drift length by placing the fly downstream of the tippet, leader, and fly line at an approximate 45-degree angle. This ensures that the fly is floating without drag for the longest time possible, as the line and leader need to catch up to it in the drift before they can pull the fly, creating drag.

Make sure that you are casting to the fish from a position upstream of it, so your presentation will be made quartering downstream. You execute a reach cast on your final casting stroke toward the fish, just before you lay the line onto the water. As your line, leader, and fly are straightening in front of you, toward your target, sweep your casting arm upstream, and then allow the line to settle to the surface. If the fly lands downstream of your line but still upstream of the fish so it has time to float to the target, you've successfully completed a reach cast.

The reach cast isn't difficult to perform, but there is some nuance involved in executing a good one. First, you need to compensate for the amount of line you're using to reach the fish. If you cast straight at a trout rising across from you, you'll use less line than if you're casting downstream at an angle with a reach cast. This causes many anglers to cast short of the fish they're targeting; they haven't compensated enough for the mending cast.

It's not always vital to mend. Here fly-casting legend Ed Jaworowski makes a perfect presentation with a straight line cast. When casting upstream into water moving toward you, simply strip in the excess line as it floats down to you to facilitate the hook set. The fly will float drag-free. There's no reason to mend from this position.

The other common problem when anglers are just developing their reach cast is that they use an aggressive, forceful motion to complete the cast. This often causes the line and fly to slam to the water, scaring the fish and usually sinking the dry fly. It takes some practice, but you're trying to achieve a smooth-motion transition from your final backcast to your reach cast, and you shouldn't apply any more force than you'd use to complete any other cast.

Curve Cast

A curve cast, just as its name implies, is intended to help you throw a curve with your fly, leader/tippet, and line, so that they don't land in a straight line on the water. Anglers use this cast so that they don't "line" a fish by having their fly line and leader float over a rising trout before their fly does, potentially scaring it. Some anglers describe this cast as being a positive or negative curve cast, depending on which way they're trying to curve the fly. But I just refer to it as curving left or curving right.

Anglers often use curve casts when conditions force them to cast directly upstream to a rising fish, and they want to kick the fly to the side of their line. But casting around in-stream obstructions like logs or boulders can also require a curve cast. It's always better to move to a new position to get into the best casting situation for any particular fish. But this isn't always possible. Perhaps the water is too deep for you to wade into a better spot, or maybe it's streamside vegetation or a cliff wall that inhibits you from moving.

The most important thing to remember when executing any cast is that the fly line, and ultimately your fly, will follow whatever you do with your rod tip at the end of your casting stroke. There are multiple ways to achieve the curve cast. I'll discuss the easiest to learn first, and then a more difficult, but very effective, alternative.

The easiest way to perform a curve cast is to drop the tip of your rod out to your side, more parallel to the ground than near your head. Which side will depend on whether you're trying to curve the line to the left or right. Dip the rod tip to your right side to make the line curve left, and dip it to the left to curve right. Now sweep the rod tip in a casting stroke toward your opposite side. But stop abruptly when the rod tip passes in front of you. This will cause the line and fly to curve at the end of the cast, continuing in the arc you created before stopping the stroke abruptly.

The easy curve cast requires that you have enough room to your left or right to create the backcast that instigates the curve. But what if you don't have enough room? There's another way to complete the curve: by twisting your wrist at the end of the cast.

Here's how to execute this more challenging cast: Keep your rod tip more vertical (near your head), like any normal cast, and then cycle the cast forward. As your line is straightening in front of you and you're just about to

Ed Jaworowski implements a perfect curve cast to present his fly on the opposite side of the fast water while not spooking any fish that may be living there. Curving the fly in the direction of the hand in which you're holding your rod (curve right for right-handers, left for left-handers) is difficult at first, but it can be mastered with practice.

let it begin to settle to the water, twist your wrist. If you twist it to the right, the fly will curve to the left. And if you twist left (much more difficult to master for a right-handed caster), it will curve to the right.

The curve cast is more difficult to execute than the reach cast, but all it takes is practice. My friend Walt Young throws one of the most beautiful curve casts I've witnessed. Many years ago, we would hang out at the fly shop he was managing and practice making curve casts around the outside trash cans. Practice this cast, and someday it will pay off by helping you fool a difficult trout in a difficult spot.

Puddle or Pile Cast

The puddle cast (also called the pile cast) is a great tool for acquiring a downstream, drag-free drift when swift-moving or conflicting currents make it difficult to achieve. The idea with this cast is to allow the end of your

Matt Grobe implements a puddle cast to get the longest possible drift in the slack water beneath the tree. Notice how Matt's rod tip is near the water while his fly line and leader are just beginning to fall to the surface in a puddle.

leader and all of your tippet to land in loose coils, in a puddle, with the fly floating beside them. This creates more time for the fly to float drag-free while the current straightens the coils and ultimately pulls your fly, causing it to drag.

Most of the time when you cast your dry fly to the water, you're aiming for a spot less than a foot above the water on your final stroke—high enough so that the fly doesn't slam onto the surface when you lay it down, but low enough to allow your leader to straighten. But with the puddle cast, you need to aim your rod tip higher, above the water, rather than toward it.

Begin with a low backcast (rod tip pointing toward the ground) and stop your rod tip higher than normal on the forward cast, then immediately drop your rod tip toward the water as the line straightens. Because the line always follows the rod tip, this will throw your fly higher into the air than normal and allow it to flutter down to the water's surface. This cast is very difficult to execute if it's windy because the wind will grab the fly more easily as it falls, often making your cast inaccurate. But there are places, particularly in

pocketwater, swirling backeddies, or other areas of slack current adjacent to moving water, where the puddle cast gives you the best chance to get a drag-free, fish-fooling drift.

THE MOST IMPORTANT ON-WATER MENDS

I wrote earlier in this chapter that on-water mends are not ideal for dry-fly fishing. But there are times when the only way to extend your drift is to complete an on-water mend. And there are two particular instances when these mends are vital to getting a good drift or extending one.

Most anglers struggle to keep from sinking their dry flies when attempting on-water mends. It takes practice to get it right like Taylor Depauw does here, using just enough force to complete the mend without drowning his fly.

The first important on-water mend is performed by moving only the part of your fly line that is being pulled by the current and repositioning it either up- or downstream, to counteract the pull. This is often necessary when you're casting longer distances across varying currents. The vast majority of the time you'll conduct this mend by lowering your rod tip toward the water and then flipping as much of the line as necessary upstream until your fly is no longer dragging. You may have to do this several times throughout the drift if the water is moving quickly. But if you're standing in an eddy that is moving much slower than the water where your dry fly is floating, you may have to flip some of your line downstream to achieve the same goal. The key is using only as much force as necessary to move just the portion of your line that's causing your fly to drag. It takes practice to not pull all of your line and move or sink your fly. I believe that longer (10-foot) dry-fly rods make this mend much easier to employ because they use a longer lever to do so. But it can be completed with any rod.

The other on-water mend that's vital for dry-fly fishing is shaking your line to extend a drift. If you've been dry-fly fishing for any period of time, you've probably cast to a fish only to see it rise again farther downstream than you expected. Or maybe your fly floated past one fish without being eaten, and you'd like it to keep floating to a fish that's rising farther downstream. The best way to do this is by shaking line.

The key to shaking line to extend your drift is, again, using the proper amount of force to make it happen. Shake too hard and you'll sink the fly. Shake too gently and the line won't come out fast enough. You can extend the drift by moving the rod tip back and forth in front of you, allowing the water's surface tension to pull the line so that it comes out of the rod tip. But before you do this, you'll need to pull enough line off your reel to allow it to smoothly slide out of the guides. Make sure to always keep the line between your finger and your rod's grip as the line slowly glides into the water. That way if a fish unexpectedly eats your fly while you're shaking line, you can still hook it by simply clamping down on the line and raising the rod tip.

WHERE TO PLACE THE CAST IN RELATION TO THE FISH

I had a rather surly guide the first time I went fly fishing for bonefish in Andros, Bahamas. He was the kind of guide an expert loves—he puts you on the fish—but he made it very tough for a beginner. We approached the first tailing bonefish I had ever seen, and the guide said, "Cast, man, cast!" No other instruction. Casting to a tailing bonefish is very similar to dry-fly fishing: you can see the fish feeding, or at least part of the fish, and making an accurate cast is very important.

I said, "Cast where?" The guide was flabbergasted. "You don't see that fish, man?" I could see only part of its tail poking through the water. Where was its head? Where was I supposed to cast? You might have the right dry fly tied to your leader and a trout rising in front of you, but if you don't make the correct cast, you'll have as much success as I had with that first bonefish. Your position in relation to a rising fish is often the key component in whether you'll be able to get a drag-free drift with your dry fly.

Upstream Position

I prefer to cast a dry fly to a trout rising in flat water from a position slightly upstream of it. This casting position, combined with a reach cast, is the most effective way to have your fly float drag-free. It's also the best way to get your fly to the trout before your leader and fly line reach it. You don't need to be more than a few feet upstream from the fish for this to work. The cast becomes more problematic to execute well the farther upstream you move, and this enhances the probability that your fly will drag before reaching your target. Solid hook sets are also much more difficult to make as the distance increases.

Anglers tend to pull their flies out of a fish's mouth more on upstream presentations than any other casting position, so you need to pause before you set the hook. After a trout rises and eats your fly, it will then begin to descend, settling back to its original holding position below the water's surface. Don't lift your rod tip to set the hook until the fish closes its mouth and begins to descend. If you set too early, you'll pull your fly right out of the fish's mouth before it has the chance to close its jaws; you'll lift and come up empty.

The importance of waiting for the fish to settle before setting the hook is magnified in some situations and for some trout species. Trout that are lazily gliding through a pool, picking off trapped flies like mayfly spinners or spent caddis, often feed very slowly. It's easy to miss the hook set with fish feeding this way. Cutthroat trout are also famous for rising painfully slow to your fly, making the angler antsy and often causing a quick hook set that fails.

Some anglers force themselves to utter a quick sentence like "God save the queen" or "Set the hook now" before they lift, to remind themselves to pause. That's never worked particularly well for me, so I don't do it. I'm usually too engrossed in watching the fish feed to remember to say anything. But it might work for you, so give it a try. I just wait for the fish to feed and then settle, and that works great, too.

Even with the Fish

Sometimes deep water or bankside obstructions stop you from getting upstream from the trout, and you have to cast from a position directly across from it. This casting position creates several problems. First, you still must be able to get your fly upstream of the fish to allow it to float down to it. But if you try to do this by casting right at the fish, you may drop your fly line right on its head, often provoking it to stop rising. There are a couple of ways to combat this.

The reach cast is vital here. But you'll have to increase the reach by exaggerating the sweeping motion at the end of your cast to get the fly farther upstream. And you'll need to compensate for the increased distance by shooting more fly line. Anglers trying to shoot their casts higher upstream

Cutthroat trout like this one are notorious for rising very slowly and deliberately before taking a dry fly. Watching a big cuttie slowly rise in clear water from the stream bottom toward your dry takes a lot of self-control; you must not pull the fly from the fish's mouth before it has a chance to eat it.

in this manner also tend to drop the fly line from their off hand (the hand not holding the rod) as they make their final cast. But if you do this, the line will often wrap around the butt of your rod or your stripping guide, or you'll end up with too much slack line between you and the fish, impeding your ability to set the hook. Make a loop between your index finger and your thumb and allow the line to slide through it as you finish the cast. This helps you maintain line control as it shoots to the fish.

You can also employ a curve cast to try to get the fly to the fish without throwing your leader and line on top of it. But, again, you'll need to adjust your casting distance to throw your line past the fish before curving it. Even if you execute this cast well, you're going to place your fly line near the fish. This can frighten the trout if it's rising in calm water. It's best to use the curve cast from this position only if you're casting into a riffle where the broken current can obscure your line.

Downstream Position

There are a few instances where casting to a trout from a position downstream of it can be beneficial. But it's also very easy to frighten a rising fish when casting from below it because you'll often have to cast your line and leader very close to it. Again, riffles help to mitigate the chances of frightening the trout, as the broken water tends to obscure your line. I usually try to cast from this position only if I'm blind casting dries into riffled water.

But there will be times when you are forced to cast from a downstream position in flat water. This is where the curve cast becomes a tremendous aid. You can place your line farther from the fish, reducing the chances of frightening it, if your fly has curved into its feeding lane away from your line. But only try this as a last resort. The opportunity for failure here is much larger than if you're upstream of the trout. Many anglers cast from below the fish in flat water only because they're too lazy to move from the spot where they're already standing. The best course is usually to walk to the bank behind you, very slowly and cautiously, and then move to a position upstream of the fish to present your fly.

The downstream casting position does give an angler one big advantage for setting the hook: it's much easier to pull your fly into the fish's mouth when you're setting the hook from below it, rather than pulling the fly away from the fish if you're upstream of it.

CASTING A FLY TANDEM

I included a category in the fly pattern style charts (chapter 4) that described each style's effectiveness for use in a tandem. A fly tandem is made from two flies connected to each other, fished at the same time. The charts consider only tandems comprising a nymph floating beneath a dry fly. But tandems with two dry flies can also be very effective. Perhaps you want to use a less visible dry fly tied below one that's easy to see to help you find it on the water. Or maybe you just want to give the fish options: a large dry with a smaller one, an aquatic insect with a terrestrial, or a flashy dry tied from synthetic materials with a more muted pattern.

Charlie Meck wrote a terrific book dedicated to this topic called *Fishing Tandem Flies*. In it, he describes several ways to tie a tandem. But most of the time I just connect my tandems with a separate piece of monofilament tippet. I tie the lead fly to my leader and then cut another piece of tippet to form the tandem. The length of this tippet is determined by the depth of the water you're fishing if you're using it to attach a nymph. But if I'm adding another dry fly, I want the tippet to be long enough that the flies are separated when they land on the water, but not so far apart that it becomes difficult to see both of them simultaneously. I usually use a tippet section approximately 2 to 3 feet long.

This angler is slightly upstream of the trout rising in front of the sticks in the photo's bottom right corner. He is in an ideal position to catch a trout rising in this flat, calm water. The upstream casting position, combined with a reach cast and the ability to gently shake the line to extend the drift as needed, makes an angler a very effective dry-fly fisher.

I take this tippet and tie a clinch knot around my index finger at one end. I begin to pull the knot tight but stop when I have formed a small loop. I then pass the point of the hook from the fly tied to my leader through this loop and pull the knot tight. The tippet is now hanging from the bend of my lead fly's hook, and I tie my second fly to the end of it, completing the tandem.

Anglers encounter a couple of difficulties when casting and fishing tandems. First, you must adjust the length of your cast for fishing along a bank. Both flies shouldn't land tight to the streambank; if they do, they're most likely tangled. You need to recognize that you're casting to where the *bottom* fly in the tandem will land. If you cast too far, the bottom fly will often become tangled in bankside vegetation. It's also very easy to tangle these two flies as you cast when you're just learning to fish a tandem.

Most fly fishers strive for tight loops when they cast. That means that they want both the top and bottom of the fly line loop to be close together in the air to cut through wind and to add distance to the cast. But you don't want tight loops when fishing fly tandems or you'll tangle the flies. You need to cast with an open loop. The easiest way to open your loops is to press your thumb into your cork grip on your forward stroke and to slightly dip your rod on your backcast. Both of these movements dip the tip of your rod. Because the line always follows the rod tip, dipping the tip will open your loops and allow the flies to pass each other in the air without tangling.

7

Tactics for Large and Difficult Trout

CRUCIAL POINTS
- Large or difficult trout often require an individualized plan to catch them.
- Trout sometimes surface feed in unique ways that make them more difficult to catch.
- The rule of three casts will help you to know when to keep casting and when to try something different.

Large trout are an oft-stated goal for many anglers. But what is a large trout? A large trout may be only 6 inches long in a small, relatively sterile headwater stream. Most anglers consider a 20-inch river fish to be a large trout. But a 15-inch fish isn't exactly small. A friend who often fishes the Upper Delaware River once told me that if he ever becomes bored catching 15-inch trout, he'll quit fishing. And I agree with him.

A river or stream's largest trout, not matter how big they are, usually have a few things in common. They generally occupy the best holding water because they're able to force out smaller fish, though the water that a large trout finds ideal might not always seem that way to you. They can be anywhere, but there are some obvious places you should spend extra time searching for them: scum or bubble lines along pools; shaded areas beneath bankside vegetation; in deep water beside structure such as fallen trees, boulders, or ledges that divide it from shallow water; and backeddies, particularly if they're creating fish-obscuring foam on the surface.

Large trout are often careful to not show themselves to overhead predators while they feed. Search for them early in the morning and right before dark in areas with water deep enough to cover a big fish. But know that sometimes this water doesn't have to be as deep as you might think. Large fish will

Having someone spot fish from a higher vantage point can help you determine the size of the fish you see rising. The spotter can also inform you of any reaction from the fish and advise whether you're casting to the proper place. Just make sure your spotter isn't easily seen, or the fish may flee.

A large trout caught with a dry fly is considered the highest achievement possible for some fly anglers. But big fish aren't common in every waterway, and it can sometimes require a lot of searching to find one. Spend time looking for the type of cover where a big fish may live—scum lines, backeddies, deep pools—if large fish are your goal.

often move into very shallow riffles or tails of pools to feed during a hatch, particularly during low-light conditions.

You'll probably have to make some fishing sacrifices as you pursue large trout. It often means you'll have to spend more time looking and less time casting. Your pace may need to quicken, even during a hatch, while you're searching for them. That's because you're probably going to have to ignore smaller fish in easy holding areas to find big fish. If you get stuck trying to catch the little guys, you'll probably run out of time to look for the big ones. They'll be fewer in number and sometimes living far from one another, so you'll have to keep moving until you find one.

Once you find one, it'll usually be more difficult to catch because it's probably encountered a lot of anglers and their artificial flies during its life, before you arrived. This is particularly true of easily reached, famous trout water near urban populations. Now, you'll need to slow your pace while you're trying to catch a big fish. Be determined to catch it, even if your friends are catching more fish than you by targeting small ones. It'll probably take some time to find the right dry fly and the correct drift before the fish eats. Big trout have usually learned a few tricks along the way that have helped them live long enough to attain their size.

How do you know for sure when you've found a large rising fish? It seems like a simple question, but it's not always an easy thing to do. Obviously, if you can climb a bank above a fish in clear water and watch it rise without spooking it, you'll get a good idea of how large it is. But this isn't always possible. Sometimes, a trout will stick enough of its head out of the water when it feeds that you'll be able to gauge its size: big head usually equals big fish. An opportunity to guess a fish's size is also created when a trout eats a fly just beneath the surface and shows part of its head, back, and tail. The more time that passes from when you first see the fish's head break the surface to when you last see part of its tail, generally the longer this fish is. This can be difficult to gauge at first, though you will get better with practice.

One of the reasons big, wild, rising fish aren't always easy to discern is that they sometimes rise like little fish. Some of the largest rising trout I've caught made only very subtle dimples on the surface as they ate. One particularly memorable fish I caught was on the edge of a riffle in the Upper Delaware River's Main Stem a few miles upstream of Callicoon, New York. This fish never showed itself when it fed. It simply hovered beneath floating mayfly duns and gently sucked them subsurface. I wasn't sure what I was seeing when I first noticed the strangely disappearing mayflies. But after watching several insects disappear, a faint glimpse of the fish's snout became my target.

Perhaps the most difficult riseform to determine fish size is the gulping boil. I've been streamside many times, particularly when large flies were on the water, and often near dusk or after dark, when an aggressively feeding fish sounded like someone flushing a toilet as it grabbed insects from the surface. Sometimes this is an indication of a large rising trout. But not always. The sound is caused by water displacement, and that can be performed by the body of a large trout pushing water. But it can also occur when midsize fish jettison aggressively to the surface to feed, pushing the water with the side of their bodies as they return to their starting position once the insect is captured.

Of course, there is no such thing as "always" in fly fishing. I once discovered a dimpling trout making only the smallest disturbance as it picked Hendrickson mayflies from the water's surface; I was sure it was a monster. But when I finally was able to get this fish to eat my dry fly, he was so small that I threw him over my shoulder, onto dry land, with my hook set. I found him and put him back in the river. But I felt badly about that one.

The Upper Delaware Main Stem is famous for its pods of cruising trout. Chasing these fish is seldom effective. You can also frighten them with your line if you start casting before you know where they are. It's usually best to wait, be patient and ready to cast, when you see them in your casting range.

CRUISING TROUT

Chasing cruising fish is one of the biggest traps for dry-fly anglers. A cruising fish is one that doesn't hold its position by feeding repeatedly in the same place. On the Upper Delaware River's Main Stem, pods of rainbows will sometime cruise together, rising every few feet as they work their way downriver. Some anglers pull their boat anchor and try to follow the fish downstream. But this seldom works and often leads to scaring all the trout until they quit rising. These cruising fish often move in a distinct pattern. They will feed down to a certain spot, turn around, return to near where they started feeding, and then complete the process again. The best way to catch them is to remain stationary. Let the fish come to you. Make a cast when they are above you, another when they're even with the boat, and one as they're moving past. Then patiently wait for them to return.

Other trout, often large, solitary fish, cruise in a mostly haphazard way, plucking one fly here and another over there without stopping at all. You should decide immediately whether catching a fish that's feeding this way is important to you, because you might spend all your time trying to catch it instead of catching a bunch of trout that are feeding in rhythm from one spot. If it's a big cruising trout, it'd probably be important to me to try to catch it.

The first thing I do is stop casting and observe what the fish is doing. Is there any pattern to where the fish is feeding, any repetition of movement that might allow you to move to an ambush point to wait for the fish to rise near you? If there is, then move to that spot. I'll sometimes walk slowly back to the shore to enable me to move quickly on dry land, up- or downriver without scaring the fish, to get into a good casting position for the next time it feeds near me.

If you're unable to anticipate the spot the fish will be rising next and you're running out of time to try to get lucky with a random cast, then it's time to take extreme measures. I've had some luck by intentionally casting my dry fly on top of the last rise the fish has made. This will sometimes invoke a predatory strike that causes the fish to eat your fly. At other times, this might scare the fish into no longer rising. That's why this is an extreme measure, one you should take only when you're out of other options.

ONE-AND-DONE TROUT

Trout that rise once, eat something from the surface, and then disappear are the most difficult to catch. I call these fish "one-and-done" trout. You need to understand why trout do this to fully grasp why they are so frustrating for dry-fly fishermen and why, for the most part, you should ignore them and move on.

One-and-done fish have already proven to you that they are in the mood to feed. They just did that. But they haven't really shown you where they are holding after they feed and where they're going to surface feed next—if they surface feed again. Maybe they are still holding right where they just ate. Or maybe they moved a little. Perhaps they moved a lot. And exactly what did the fish eat? Unless you were extremely lucky and happened to be staring at the spot the fish rose, you probably can't be certain. And even then, you might not know. It's nearly impossible to make an accurate cast if you don't know exactly where the fish is holding and quite likely that you'll frighten it by inadvertently casting on top of it. And if you don't know what the fish ate, what fly should you cast to it?

These fish are different than cruising trout. Cruising trout move around, seldom eating at the exact spot from one rise to another. But they are in a pattern of eating from the surface; one-and-done trout are not. Cruising fish also tend to do so when there are natural flies on the water. But sometimes you can't see anything on the surface when a one-and-done fish eats. And that's part of the problem.

One-and-done trout are a time trap. The chances that you'll catch one of them are much slimmer than for a stationary rising trout, a cruising fish, or even fish that you might find by blind casting nearby. But it can be tough to ignore a one-and-done trout when you get a good look at it and it's big. Now you really want to catch it. I've had guiding clients that I nearly had to drag away from one-and-done fish that they *knew* would eat their fly on the

One-and-done trout, those that feed once on the surface and then disappear, are nearly impossible to pattern in terms of where they will rise next, *if* they rise again. An angler who tries to catch one knows where the fish was but is uncertain whether it remained there or moved to another spot. These trout are a time trap and best avoided if you want to increase your odds of catching fish.

very next cast, even though they hadn't seen the fish in 20 minutes and were casting the whole time.

This is another good reason for solidly forming your expectations for the day, and then making a decision as to whether you want to spend your valuable fishing time casting to a trout that you're more than likely not going to catch, or searching for a more cooperative fish. Part of this troubling equation is that every once in a while you will catch one of these unicorns, setting you up to get trapped by the next one.

The one-and-done trout that you just saw rise may have eaten something from the surface; you believe it must have because you saw it near the surface. But you probably didn't get a good look, because you weren't really expecting to see that fish and it rose only once. The first thing I do when I decide to try to catch one of these trout is to add a sunken dropper to my dry fly.

Many times, a one-and-done fish hasn't really taken something floating on top of the water. It was grabbing something just beneath the surface, like an emerging aquatic insect or a drowned terrestrial. Or maybe the fish just tried to eat a pine needle that fell from a tree. Trout learn what to eat by tasting things and spitting out items that aren't food. That's why they'll sometimes eat cigarette butts or your fly. And sometimes that's the reason they rise only once: they are just checking out an item they think could be food.

But what if the fish really did just eat an actual insect? Without certainty for your approach, the best course of action is to cover multiple options. You do that by casting a dry/nymph tandem rig to the place you saw the fish rise. The flies I'll most often use are ones that have caught other trout recently—or ones that imitate aquatic insects or terrestrials that could be found on the water at that time of year, even though I may not currently see them. So if it's the time of year when Sulphur mayflies hatch, tie on a Sulphur dry fly with a Sulphur nymph as your dropper. Or try to cover multiple options by using a Sulphur dry and dropping a sunken ant off of it. Whatever you do, keep at least one eye on the rest of the water around you, and look for a fish that's easier to catch. That is probably your best option when confronted with a one-and-done trout.

DIFFICULT TROUT

It's not always easy to quantify what an angler means when they describe a rising trout as difficult to catch. Obviously, it means that the angler had

Achieving a drag-free drift while casting dry flies over heavy current seams can be difficult. A longer rod can help keep most of your line off the water and assist with drag. Here, Matt Grobe is hooked up with a cutthroat trout that thought it was safe to eat in its tricky feeding lane.

more trouble than usual catching it. But a difficult fish for one angler may be easier for another. When you first start fishing dry flies, the fish are all tough to catch. I place difficult fish in one of two categories: those that are

Trout that live in flat, glassy pools with little current are some of the most difficult to catch, particularly if the fish are wild and the food supply is abundant, like on the Upper East Branch of the Delaware River.

difficult because of what they are eating, and those that are difficult because of where they are eating.

Fish in the "what they are eating" group may be difficult because they are rising only to small insects that are hard for you to see. Or maybe they've keyed into a natural insect's single physical trait, and they are unable to be caught until you figure out what that is. I've witnessed difficult fish pick out only mayfly duns that the wind has knocked over onto their sides. I've seen them focus their attention solely on mayfly spinners that shudder as they're dying, creating small wakes on the water's surface, and ignore the ones that aren't moving. Maybe they're the only fish in a stream section eating the nonobvious masking hatch occurring simultaneously with an obvious hatch: picking out sparse, occasional little Sulphur duns during a heavy Green Drake emergence.

The only way I was able to crack those codes was to briefly quit trying to catch those difficult trout and closely observe the things happening around me. Bending over at the waist to more intensely scrutinize insects on the water's surface can help. So can shining a light on the water, away from the fish so as not to scare it, if it's near or after dark. But if your dries are being ignored when you know you're making good, drag-free casts, particularly if other fish nearby have eaten your fly, then the only option is to stop, try to observe exactly how the fish is feeding and what it's eating, recalibrate, and cast again, probably with a different fly.

Trout in the "where they are eating" category of being difficult are the most problematic to catch for a few reasons. Maybe you just don't have the skills today to place your fly in a spot or manner in which the fish will eat it. But I can guarantee that if you don't try to catch it today, you won't have the skills to catch it tomorrow either. Consider it practice. Don't ignore trout rising in tough places because you're afraid you'll lose your fly. Many anglers do, and that gives you an advantage if you're bold enough to try and sometimes fail.

The first house my wife and I owned sat above a trout stream with a good population of wild brown trout. This was my best classroom for improving as a dry-fly angler. The stream was tree lined and fish would often rise close to the banks, several feet beneath overhanging tree limbs. The first few times I found trout rising under the trees, I ignored them. Why would I want to get my line, leader, and fly stuck in the trees and waste what little fishing time I had trying to untangle it all?

That approach was fine for me until the day that the only rising fish I could find were all beneath those tree limbs. So I decided to go for it. My first cast became so tangled in the branches that I scared all the rising fish while trying to extricate my gear. I was disappointed and went home. The next time this happened I made the same terrible cast into the tree, got stuck again, and had to retie everything. But I handled it differently this time. I went back to where I had first attempted to cast, without tying a new fly to my leader, and I practiced casting under those trees, even though the fish had long since quit rising. And I made a couple of casts that would have worked.

Every time I fished that stream section after that, I cast beneath those trees until I could do it well most of the time. The whole reason those fish rose there in the first place was that few anglers ever tried to catch them—because they knew they couldn't. There is value in casting to all the places where you see fish rise, or that just look fishy, particularly if they are difficult to reach. Big fish live in these places. Most anglers are afraid to fish them. Cast into them. Get stuck. Retrieve your gear and cast into them again. Once you develop better dry-fly casting skills than most other anglers, it won't matter if they fish a stream section before you. They won't be able to reach the fish you can reach.

DECIDING WHEN TO STICK AND WHEN TO MOVE

How do you know when it's time to move on after failing to catch a specific rising fish? Or when it's time to change your fly or make other adjustments? The answers to these questions are found, once again, in the goals you've set for the day. I can sometimes be a very stubborn fisherman, and I'll often spend a great deal of time trying to catch a single large or difficult trout. I've fished with friends, more than once, who've bragged about how they outfished me because I spent so much time trying to catch one of these fish while they jumped from trout to trout, picking off the easy ones. These differing approaches highlight the decisions you sometimes need to make when you're dry-fly fishing.

If you simply want to catch as many rising fish as you can, tie on a dry fly as similar in shape and color as possible to the flies you're seeing and cast to the trout rising closest to you. The first thing I do after watching a fish eat a live insect or two is consider the type of water I'm fishing. Think about the pattern style assessments in chapters 2 and 3, and choose the style you think fits the specific water type and hatch you're encountering. If you catch the fish on your first cast, great. But if you've tried your best fly option and made a series of accurate drag-free casts and the fish still doesn't eat, move on to find an easier fish. Look for one that's close to you, in a spot where you're most comfortable acquiring a drag-free drift with a manageable cast.

But know that if you don't test yourself at times by trying to catch the most difficult fish, you probably won't learn anything, and you won't improve as a dry-fly fisherman. I find rising trout that I can't catch within a few casts to be especially interesting. When I encounter one of these difficult trout, I begin a process of elimination to try to catch it. Here's how I advise anglers to progress.

A PLAN OF ATTACK FOR A RISING TROUT

If a trout is rising within an established rhythm, more than two times in one spot, it should provide an angler a good opportunity to catch it. If the fish isn't the first rising trout you've encountered and you've already caught one, begin by using the fly that caught the previous fish. If it's the first fish you've encountered, spend a brief period studying the water to see what might be hatching. Then study the fish's riseform—is it sipping, bulging, splashing? Riseforms can help you decide what the fish might be eating. Once you believe you know what the fish is eating, use the fly that matches it as closely as possible.

This next step is very important. A lot of anglers, with a fly now tied to their leader and a fish rising in front of them, are so excited that they start casting. But don't do that just yet. Let the fish rise again and be sure to mark its location as accurately as possible. Slowly move into your best casting

Successful dry-fly anglers stop, observe, and think about their approach as they study the water before casting to a rising fish. They can then adjust their leader and tippet as necessary and choose the best fly for the job. Patience is paramount.

position, and then let the trout rise once more. I generally like to be slightly upstream of the fish so that I'm casting with a downstream angle.

Now you and the fish are both holding in set positions. Cast your dry fly to the fish, placing the fly approximately 1 to 3 feet upstream of it, depending on the type of water you are fishing. Flatter water often requires a longer drift for a fish to take your fly. Make sure you are using a reach cast (see chapter 5) to place your fly downstream of the leader and fly line, achieving the longest drag-free drift. Cast no more than three times to the trout as long as each cast covers the area where the fish is feeding with a drag-free drift.

Make sure your fly floats a foot or so downstream of the trout before you pick it up to recast. If you make a poor cast that doesn't cover the fish, you should also wait until your fly, leader, and line pass downstream of the fish before recasting. Many anglers are impatient, and they'll tear their fly line from the water in front of the fish to cast again. You might get away with doing that occasionally, but sooner or later you'll scare a rising trout you really wanted to catch.

If the fish doesn't take your fly after the third cast, do not cast again just yet. Wait. Watch for insects that are floating over the fish and observe what the fish eats when it rises again. If the fish quits rising, you might have scared it with a bad cast, it might have moved, or maybe it just stopped surface feeding for the moment. Once you are reasonably sure the fish is gone, find another one and begin this process again.

If the fish rises again, begin your sequence of three drag-free casts before stopping and watching again. Complete this sequence until you are reasonably sure that the fish is not going to take your fly as currently presented. When your casting grows increasingly panicked as you're failing to catch the fish rising around you during a hatch, the worst thing you can do is to keep casting.

What happens next will depend on what other fish have done before you cast to this one. If you have caught other rising fish nearby with the fly that's currently tied to your leader, remain patient before switching patterns, and attempt several more three-cast sequences, waiting for the fish to rise again after each one. But if this is the first rising fish you've tried to catch and it has either ignored or refused your fly, then it's time to make a change.

A fish refuses a fly when it swims up to it like it's going to eat it but doesn't. Sometimes trout refuse flies with a great swirl and splash, making you believe they ate your fly, but when you set the hook, there's nothing there. A refusal is a better response from a trout than just ignoring your fly. Trout don't want to waste valuable energy resources by swimming toward food they're not going to eat. So if your fly grabbed the fish's attention enough for it to take a look, you and the pattern did a lot of things correctly, just not everything. Perhaps the fly dragged slightly just as it reached the fish. Try another cast to achieve a better drift. But maybe the problem was that the fly didn't move enough.

Fish can sometimes key into insect movement, particularly during hatches of large insects like Drakes and stoneflies, when fly patterns can more easily be discerned as forgeries. Consider long-lasting hatches like those of Eastern Sulphurs and Western PMDs; if the fish are constantly being presented with similar drag-free dry flies, day after day, they may want to see the fly move before eating it. So it's now time to impart a brief, gentle movement into the fly.

Cast approximately 2 feet upstream of the rising fish and once the fly lands, pull your fly line very gently to make it move just a little. Most anglers will pull too hard at first, causing the fly to sink or even dragging it away from the fish's feeding lane. But you'll get better with practice.

After you have twitched the fly in front of the trout, you want it to float drag-free by the time it reaches the fish. So when your fly is about a foot from the fish, throw a little slack into your cast by wiggling your rod tip to feed some line onto the water (see chapter 5). This removes the tension from the drift and allows the fly to float freely again.

If the fish has been completely ignoring your fly, rather than refusing it, it's time to try something else. You could add more tippet length or a lighter tippet if you feel your drifts aren't good enough. This can sometimes help when the fish are refusing your flies, but it's seldom the answer when your dry is being completely ignored.

If moving your fly and adding finer tippet fails to catch the fish, it's time to stop fishing and observe again. What have you missed? Is there more than

If the rising trout you're trying to catch doesn't eat your fly, wait till it floats well below your target before recasting. This is particularly important in flat, clear water, such as pictured here. Plucking your fly from the water too close to a rising trout can frighten the fish, causing it to quit feeding.

one insect hatching (often called a masking hatch)? If so, try a pattern to imitate the insect you just noticed and begin your three-cast series again.

If you aren't finding more than one type of insect on the water, then maybe the fish is keying in on a specific facet of the insect you're trying to imitate. Is it eating emergers? Is it taking a spinner that's falling while others are hatching, or vice versa? Is there something else you're missing, like cripples (flies that look different than others by lying on their sides)? If you believe that any of these things are possible, try to find a fly in your box that imitates this specific attribute, or alter your existing fly to match (cut the wings off, twist the hackle so it lands on its side, etc.).

If the fish is clearly eating insects that look like your fly but won't eat yours, try another pattern style in the same size that also matches the hatch. Sometimes fish see a particular fly style too often, and they begin to ignore it. So if you've been using a size 14 yellow Compara-dun, try another style, like a size 14 yellow Catskill fly or whatever alternative you have available. This is why many hatch-matching dry-fly specialists carry multiple dry flies to imitate the same hatch. Sometimes it's because one style works better on one type of water—flat vs. broken water, for instance—but often it's just to have options for difficult fish. Begin another three cast series with your new fly pattern style and proceed through the previously described steps from there.

If this doesn't work, it may be time to try a different size of the same pattern. If the hatch you're fishing is sparse and the fish is rising in flat water, you should drop the fly pattern one size and begin again. So instead of using a size 14 yellow bug, try a size 16. Fish the fly with a drag-free drift just as you did when you started fishing your initial pattern. If the hatch is heavy and you think your fly just isn't standing out among the myriad of naturals, if

Large aquatic insects are difficult to imitate with artificial flies because the fish can easily see them as forgeries. This sometimes induces trout to want to see a fly move before it eats it—proof of life. You may need to impart some movement to your dries to fool a difficult trout into eating a large mayfly like this Yellow Drake (*Ephemera varia*).

Sometimes it's not always clear what the fish are eating. In this photo, there's a Blue-Winged Olive cripple on the water surrounded by adult midges and empty midge pupal shucks. A fish feeding here could be eating any of these things. The only way to tell is to observe. If you're still not sure, just try a fly that matches one of them. And then try something else if that doesn't work.

you're fishing broken water like a riffle, or if darkness is quickly approaching, you may want to try a fly one size larger than the one you've been fishing. So tie on a size 12 yellow bug instead of the size 14. Begin another three cast series with your new fly and proceed through the previously described steps from there.

If you've tried all of these things and still haven't caught the fish, you're running out of options. The next thing to try is changing the angle you're casting to the fish. First, try to get closer. You might be surprised how close you can wade to a fish if you move very slowly and quietly. Wait to see the fish rise, and as it's making a disturbance on the surface, take a slow step toward the fish. Wait for it to rise again, then step toward it again. You can keep doing this as long as the fish keeps rising. If it stops rising, stop moving. Wait for it to rise and then begin casting. You can also try to cross the water you're fishing, well up- or downstream of the fish so you don't spook it, to change your angle by casting from the opposite side. Begin another three cast series from your new position and proceed through the previously described steps from there.

If this still doesn't work, it's time to try something completely different. If you've been casting a dry fly that imitates an aquatic insect, try a terrestrial. This is a long-established tactic during the West Branch of the Upper

You're not going to catch every rising fish you encounter. No one does that. But if you've exhausted your pattern selection and techniques and the fish is still rising when you leave it, at least you can take solace in the fact that your casting and presentation didn't frighten the fish. That's a good start, and it will ultimately lead to success.

Delaware's legendary Sulphur hatch. Old-timers will tell you that the best dry fly for imitating the Delaware's size 16 Sulphurs is sometimes a size 16 ant or beetle.

If this doesn't work, it's now decision time for this rising fish. For one reason or another (sometimes only the fish knows why), maybe you can't catch this fish today. If it's still rising after you've tried all these suggested tactics, then congratulations! You've done your part, and at least your fly presentations haven't scared the fish enough to make it stop rising. It may be a hollow victory, but it's a victory nonetheless.

You now have to decide if you want to be stubborn and keep trying the tactic sequences with different flies until the fish stops rising—or quit. Sometimes the next trout you try to catch, in the same pool, will eat whatever fly is now tied to your leader on the first cast. Sometimes you won't crack the code for that fish either. But it's this game that makes dry-fly fishing so fascinating. And if you've spent this much mental energy trying to catch one fish, you probably haven't been focused on all of the world's troubles. That's the real reason to fly fish anyway.

8

Rods, Reels, and Other Equipment

CRUCIAL POINTS
- Your tackle—rods, reels, fly lines, and other equipment—won't necessarily make you a better dry-fly fisherman.
- You don't have to tie your own leaders to catch fish.
- Floatants and desiccants are just as important as your rod and reel for fishing dry flies.

Anglers are often exposed to a lot of strong opinions from friends and media sources when they are learning to fly fish. This is especially true when choosing what they perceive to be the best rods, reels, lines, and leaders. Many fly-fishing beliefs are passed down over the years, from one angling authority to the next, by simply repeating what others have said. But the way in which we fish and the gear we use change over time, sometimes altering these long-held beliefs into fallacy.

RODS

Dry-fly action rods are one of these modern myths, even though you still hear this description used today. It originated from a period, long ago, when noodley bamboo wet-fly rods were still an option. These rods were very soft actioned and whippy to cast, made to roll cast a string of wet flies (called a "caste"), not to aerialize fly line for dry-fly fishing. Almost no one makes this type of rod today, and few fishermen still use them. So why do we continue to label some rods as dry-fly rods?

When most people describe a rod as having a dry-fly action, what they usually mean is that it's not as stiff as many of the "fast-action" rods currently on the market. Many anglers believe these more moderate-action rods protect the light tippets that are commonly used with dry flies. But I have

145

The best anglers are very comfortable with their favorite fly rods. But some fly fishers buy a lot of rods. That's OK, as long as you're an accomplished caster. But when you're still learning, it's best to start with one rod and make it work for you.

I love the beauty and craftsmanship of a finely made bamboo fly rod. But some of the best dry-fly fishers I know use plain, inexpensive fly rods. Your tackle won't make you a better angler. Only study, practice, and time spent on the water do that.

never found this to be true. Anglers break off fish; rods can't do anything you don't force them to do.

Any angler who yanks too hard with a soft-action rod, combined with light tippet, can break off a fish just like they can with a fast-action rod. If you get accustomed to setting the hook with a fast-action rod (which requires a more subtle rod lift to set because it transfers energy more quickly), then a fast-action rod will work fine for you. You could fish an 8-weight light saltwater fly rod during a hatch of the smallest mayflies with 6X tippet if you want to do that. It wouldn't be ideal, but you'd just need to alter how you use the rod.

I competed in a couple fly-casting distance competitions, years ago, and I purchased an extremely stiff, fast-actioned rod to facilitate these long casts. One day I found myself with some unexpected fishing time after work, but the only rod I had with me was my competition rod. I didn't like fishing with it—it really wasn't made for fishing—but after breaking off the first trout that ate my dry fly, I started setting the hook more carefully, and I caught the rest of the fish that ate my dries that night. You can make any rod work for your purposes once you understand its tolerances.

The rod action that's best for you is determined by your casting stroke and its limitations. Some anglers have type A personalities and very fast-paced, aggressive casting strokes, while others are more laid back and prefer slower rods. That said, accomplished casters can make any rod work. But even the best anglers will find that certain rods will work easier for them than others. The only way to find out which ones will be better for you is to go to a fly shop and cast a bunch of different rods. Decide which one you like best. Then fish it until you become very comfortable with it—like it's an extension of your own body.

The greatest difficulty for many anglers is that they haven't fished with a particular rod long enough to know how to properly use it. This is especially important for anglers who only get to fish a few times a year. Intermediate and beginner anglers often struggle when they switch between multiple rods without developing a feel for any of them. One of the great, yet seldom promoted, fly-fishing truths is that our casting, fishing, and catching problems are usually due to gaps in our angling skill, not our equipment.

Anglers who decide their fishing limitations are due to tackle inadequacies are often disappointed when they purchase a new rod and discover that it hasn't made them a better fly fisherman. There are lots of reasons to buy a new rod. Modern rods are beautiful, getting a new one is fun, most have lifetime guarantees if you break them, and today's rods are probably the finest ever made. Just know that buying a new rod today won't make you a better angler tomorrow. You become a better dry-fly angler by constantly learning and practicing with hard-earned stream time, not by buying new tackle.

The fly fishing industry realizes that the vast majority of anglers cannot fish as much as they'd like, so they never fully acquire the experience necessary to become great, or even good, anglers. Manufacturers try to augment our fishing inadequacies with better leader formulas, improved fly patterns, ideal fly lines, and the latest and greatest rods and reels. But these things alone cannot make you the fisherman you want to become. Lessons, time spent with anglers who are better than you, books and articles, and podcasts help you understand what's possible, but there is no substitute for experience. And this cannot be bought at any price.

I have developed my own fly-fishing tackle preferences over time. Some of my choices will be perfect for you, though you may choose to go in your own direction for others. My thoughts are just a starting point. The more you fish, the easier it will be for you to understand what you like and what you don't. Eventually, through experience, you'll acquire a tackle system that works best for you.

Dry-Fly Rod Length

The optimal length for your dry-fly rod will depend on a number of factors, some of which are determined by the way in which you prefer to fish. I generally use shorter fly rods—from 7 to 8 feet, rated for 4- or 5-weight fly lines—when I'm fishing small, tight, tree-lined streams where it's easy to tangle in overhead vegetation. I fish these shorter rods because I find that they're easier to control when I'm casting in tight quarters.

But the rise of Tenkara fishing proves that you can use longer rods on these streams if that's what you want to do. Tenkara rods have evolved from a Japanese style of fishing where an angler uses a fixed leader without a reel or traditional fly line. They can be very effective, particularly for small to medium trout. You just have to fish them differently.

You cast a Tenkara rod by simply dapping the fly in front of a rising trout or in promising-looking water. You dap the fly by using the rod to pick the line and fly from the water in front of you, then immediately cycling forward to lay them back down. False casting, where you cycle the fly back and forth in the air, isn't necessary. Tenkara rods, or even 9- or 10-foot fly rods, can be used in small streams if you dap your fly rather than cast it. There can be advantages to fishing this way. Most trout predators approach the fish from overhead, so by not aerializing fly line and waving your rod back and forth, you reduce the chances of scaring fish.

I prefer the classic fly-fishing method of using fly lines and reels because that's the way I was taught, and I simply like it better. I just try to limit my false casting in small streams. When I do false cast, I keep my line away from

I match my rod lengths to the type of water I'm fishing. I prefer longer rods, 10-footers, when I fish larger rivers and streams like Montana's big Yellowstone River.

the fish as much as possible by casting it off to the side. The only time I get the line near the fish is with my final cast, when I place the fly on the water. I also fish small streams primarily by working my way upstream. Most of the fish are facing upstream, waiting for food to flow down to them with the

In spite of the rising trend in very long but lightly lined fly rods, the most common fly rod for trout throughout the United States is still a 9-foot 5-weight. You can catch any trout swimming in the Lower 48 with a rod of that configuration.

current. I can limit my exposure and chances to spook them if I approach from behind. But I often take a different tact when fishing medium to large trout waters.

I spend most of my time fishing larger trout waters, and I usually do so with a 10-foot rod for a 5- or 6-weight line. Fifteen or 20 years ago, these long rods weren't ideal fly-fishing instruments. Most of them felt tip-heavy; the rod's weight beyond the grip made the tip feel like it wanted to fall to the water. But advancements with lighter, stronger graphite has made many long rods feel more like 9-footers in your hand; they balance well with a standard trout reel. And there are advantages to using longer rods for dry-fly fishing.

If you're fishing a large, deep river and you need to wade up to your waist to make a long cast to fish that always seem to be rising on the far side, the extra length from a 10-foot rod verses a 9-footer helps keep your backcast higher, making it less likely to hit the water behind you. But longer rods have advantages even if you're not wading deep.

Longer rods help you mend the line more effectively by giving you a physical advantage, similar to using a longer lever to move something—in this case, a fly line. A longer rod also allows the angler to keep more line off of the water. This is particularly important when casting a dry fly across conflicting currents moving at varying speeds. The less line you have on the water, the smaller the impact these currents can impart in terms of pulling your fly and making it drag. But in spite of the advantages of using longer dry-fly rods, the standard fly rod is probably still a 9-foot, 5-weight instrument. That size is used to catch rising trout all over the world. You don't need to have a 10-footer to catch fish. But you may want to try one.

Rod Material Options

Fly rods made from graphite are by far the most commonly used for modern dry-fly fishing. They range wildly in pricing, from under $100 to over $1,000. The more expensive rods will use the latest high-tech graphite, and they'll be lighter than most of their less expensive counterparts. They'll have

Dusty Smith, owner of the Livingston Rod Company, which specializes in fiberglass fly rods, used one of his creations to fool this beautiful cutthroat. Fiberglass fly rods, originally designed in the 1940s, had a strong following until they were almost completely displaced by graphite rods in the 1970s and '80s. But today's fiberglass tools are just as good as any other rod type on the market, and the material is experiencing a resurgence.

pretty reel seats, beautiful wraps, and the best line guides available. They'll also generally come with a good warranty in case you break them. But will they help you catch more fish? Not necessarily. I fish with good (meaning expensive) rods because I like them. Their beauty matches the pretty place where trout reside. But if I were looking for the best dry-fly angler on any given waterway, it might be the guy or girl whose older rod isn't as pretty because they use it all the time and they know how to make it work for them.

Fiberglass rods have made a big resurgence in recent years. Glass rods were originally invented out of necessity, when world wars caused a shortage in the raw material (Chinese Tonkin bamboo) for making bamboo fly rods. Many early glass rods were clunky, slow-actioned creations that most anglers wouldn't appreciate today. But some of these rods were good and are still in use. Modern glass rods, made today by people like my friends Dusty Smith of the Livingston Rod Company, Mike McFarland of the McFarland Rod Company, and many others have actions most anglers will appreciate. Many of these rods can be described as medium-actioned, similar to earlier generation graphite rods, which a lot of anglers find perfect for fishing dry flies. New glass rods can also vary in price, with the best usually somewhere between the cost of a mid- to high-end graphite rod.

Cane or bamboo fly rods are your final option. Many anglers consider a well-crafted cane rod to be the ultimate prize for the dry-fly fisherman. If you're in the cane rod market today, you have a lot of options. Large companies like Orvis are still making cane rods. One of their sticks will set you back $2,400 to $2,700 depending on the model. But these rods are beautifully made, and they come with a lifetime guarantee that Orvis is famous for upholding, often going beyond what they promised when you bought the rod. I own a modern Orvis 1856 cane rod, and it's a wonderful dry-fly fishing tool.

In addition to large company-made cane rods, there are hundreds of individual craftsmen around the country producing excellent rods. When my wife and I lived along Penns Creek, in Coburn, Pennsylvania, I'd spend some days hanging around Jim Downes's fly-rod shop. You can learn a lot about rod tapers and action if you spend time around one of these bamboo craftsmen. Jim gave me a hollow-built 8½-foot 6-weight when I was moving to Montana, and it's one of my favorites for tossing large foam dries.

Cane rods can be great fishing tools and they ooze the kind of history that make some fly fishermen drool. But there are a lot of them that you probably don't want to own. The old wet-fly rods I mentioned earlier, and their whippy actions, aren't ideal for casting dries. But you could do it if you wanted to. I have an old soft-action South Bend wet-fly rod that I've used with dry flies. But be aware that old cane rods need lots of work: ferrules come loose, varnish chips, guides break. And cane rods need more care than other materials.

Jim Downes, maker of the finest bamboo fly rods, shows that a cane rod is still a viable fish-catching option for dry-fly anglers. Though cane rods are often thought to be exorbitantly expensive (some are), many of today's makers charge near the same price for one as for a top-of-the-line graphite rod.

They should never be put in their tubes if they're wet. And you need to be careful to not twist their sections when putting them together and taking them apart or you'll damage the ferrules.

A cane rod will cost you anywhere from $100 for a beat-up "parts rod" to several thousand dollars (sometimes five figures) for a new rod or rare collectable. But the average new cane rod is priced similarly to the newest top-end graphite—about $1,000. Buy one because it's beautiful. Buy one because you appreciate the modern craftsman who made it. Buy one because you always wanted one, and you like how it casts. But realize that cane rods, even the best, aren't magic wands. If you want to improve your casting and catch more fish, buy yourself some lessons from a good instructor instead.

REELS AND DRAG SYSTEMS

There are two primary types of reel drag systems: disc drag and click and pawl. Most disc-drag reels use material that is pressed together as you tighten a drag knob to increase tension. The best ones have no hesitation when you

A reel with a simple or poor drag system may be fine for small trout in small water. But sooner or later you'll hook a large fish in larger water that will make you wish you had a better drag system to help you land it.

first pull line, and they feel smooth as the line is removed. Click and pawl reels have a piece of material that slides between gears to create drag. This creates tension with more of a jerking motion that can sometimes stress light tippets. However, the best click and pawl reels are smooth in their own way, and they've been successfully used for trout fishing for a very long time. You can adjust the drag tension on some click and pawl reels, but not all of them. I've heard many trout anglers state that they would never purchase a reel with a disc-drag system because the reel is only there to hold their line. These anglers believe that reels are the least important part of their trout fishing gear.

I understand this argument, though I don't completely agree with it. Sure, if you fish mainly small headwater streams for little trout, you probably don't need a disc-drag reel. Most anglers simply strip the fly line back to them to retrieve small fish. But what happens if you hook a big fish in water where there's lots of room for it to run?

I spent 10 years living along the Upper Delaware River's amazing trout fishery. Anglers in my current home state of Montana are often surprised when I tell them that I have never fished a better river system for large wild trout that often rise to dry flies than the Upper Delaware. It is a hatch matcher's paradise. The rainbows and browns average 15 inches, but this is a place where you could catch the largest river-born trout of your life on a dry fly.

Delaware River trout often reside in flat water, and they are not always easy to catch. Light tippets and large fish are a combination that often leads to break-offs and disappointment for the uninitiated Delaware fisherman. Most anglers break off fish during the hook set or on the trout's first run after taking your fly. And it's not uncommon for Delaware trout to run so far that they'll take all your fly line and leave backing pulling from your rod's tip top. Practice and familiarity with your rod are the only ways to keep from breaking off fish when you set the hook. But a good disc-drag reel will go a long way toward keeping them attached to your line for their initial runs.

There are Delaware anglers who insist on using click and pawl reels. The successful ones, just as I've said many times here, are very familiar with their tackle. They know how to "palm" their reels (putting pressure on the spool

The ability to incrementally increase your reel's drag by slowly tightening it can help protect light tippets, which is vital for landing larger fish—like this big, butter-colored brown trout—in large water.

with their hand) just enough to create extra drag force without breaking off the fish. But it takes a long time to develop this ability, and many anglers don't want to lose fish while they work on it.

I always use disc-drag reels on the Delaware, most of the time with 6X tippet for dry flies, and I seldom break off fish. The key is keeping the drag set very light for the fish's first run. You want the drag set just heavy enough to slow the fish, but not so tight that it breaks them off. After the fish's first run, many times they'll run again, but they're now getting tired. I gradually increase the tension on the drag as the fish tires and gets closer to me. You don't want to play the trout so long that you exhaust and kill them. And the whole process of gradually tightening a reel's drag can take place very quickly once you get accustomed to do it. You may live near water where the average trout isn't very big and a disc-drag reel isn't necessary. But someday you might hook the fish of a lifetime. I'd want to fight that fish with a good disc-drag reel system.

The other major choice in reel types is the way in which they're made: machined or cast. Machined reels are cut from a block of metal, most often aluminum. Cast reels are poured into a mold. Machined reels are often lighter than cast reels because they are heavily ported, which means parts of the metal are cut away to reduce weight. They are also usually more costly than cast reels because it's more complicated to make them.

Manufacturers often extoll the fact that machined reels are stronger, or less likely to break, than cast ones. But I've always thought this was an unimportant argument. I wouldn't want to drop either type, and I've never witnessed a cast reel actually fracture from a fall anyway. If I had to choose between a high-end, beautifully made machined reel without a disc drag or a less pretty cast reel with a disc drag, I'd take the reel with the better drag system every time.

FLY LINE TAPERS AND COLORS

Some anglers obsess over fly lines, especially their color. It's common in New Zealand's fabled trout waters for anglers to dye their lines to a muted shade so as not to scare the fish. I can understand how some anglers believe that a bright, fluorescent orange line flying over a fish's head could make them stop rising. But I don't believe that I've ever scared a rising trout because of my fly line's color. I believe that if you haphazardly wave a fly line of any color over a rising fish, it could scare them. But for the record, I have never fished in New Zealand, and if I spent all that time, money, and effort to get there, I'd do whatever my guide told me to do with my fly line. A good rule to always follow: do whatever the guide tells you to do.

I do believe that there is a time when brightly colored fly line is an advantage. Most fly fishermen have cast dry flies to steadily rising trout as the day's

I prefer to use lighter-colored fly lines because they help me find my fly on the water during periods of low light. Many anglers believe that light-colored lines scare fish. But this pretty cutthroat, caught in gin-clear water, didn't seem to mind the light gray fly line you can see near the top of the net.

light is quickly fading or after dark. I find that a bright line makes it a little easier for me to see where my fly is landing when daylight is running out. And this helps me to ensure that my dry fly is floating in the fish's feeding lane. It's much easier to do this with a brightly colored line than one with a muted earth tone.

There are many types of fly lines available on the market today. And just like the way in which dry-fly anglers debate their color, you'll find the same debates in relation to fly line type. The most common dry-fly lines today are weight forward. Weight-forward lines have a thin running line where they attach to the backing, and they then taper out toward the end you attach to your leader. Weight-forward lines, just as their name implies, put much of the lines' weight out front to help turn over your leader at distance, though you can use them on small streams, too.

It's getting more difficult to find double-taper lines in most fly shops. Double-taper lines are thickest at the line's center and then taper to both ends. Anglers who prefer double-taper lines often do so because of their

It really doesn't matter whether you choose to fish traditional hand-tied leaders or mass-manufactured knotless leaders. Both will do the job just fine. But I prefer knotless leaders. That way the only knot that could break is the one I use to tie on my fly. It's this angler's skill that will determine the success of the leader she's replacing, not how it was manufactured.

longevity and a belief that they present flies more subtly. When one end of a double-taper line wears out, you can just turn it over on your reel so that you're fishing the other end. You save money this way, and most of the double-taper lines cast just as well as a weight-forward at short to medium distances.

Another common trend these days is to get fly lines that are rated a half to one full line size heavier than your rod is rated—so a 5½-weight or 6-weight line for a 5-weight rod. These lines have become increasingly popular as fly rods have become increasingly stiffer and faster actioned, making good cast timing more difficult to feel and achieve for the average angler. I've never been a fan of these lines because they always feel too heavy to me. If your 5-weight rod is too fast for your casting stroke, then maybe it's not the right rod for you. Bring your own reel and line with you when you're testing fly rods. And try to cast as many rods as possible before you buy one. That way, you won't have to purchase an extra-heavy fly line to make your expensive new fly rod functional.

The biggest fly line trend in the last 10 or so years is textured lines. These lines are created with either ridges on their surface or a pattern stamped into them to reduce friction as the line slides along the guides. This reduced friction helps the line glide more easily through the guides, allowing anglers to cast farther more easily. I've used most of the textured lines on the market at one time or another and I generally like them, but they are different than traditional, smooth fly lines and some of the differences aren't helpful.

The first mass-produced textured lines could cut your wet fingers during a fishing session if you weren't careful. This isn't as big a problem with the newest textured lines because manufacturers have taken steps to mitigate the effect. But these lines are still more likely to wear on your fingers than traditional lines. Textured lines also make noise when you cast, and some anglers hate it. I've found that textured lines tend to hold more water than traditional lines, and this can lead to your guides freezing quicker if you're fishing in cold weather. Textured lines can also change the way your rod functions. The reduced friction caused by these lines tends to bend the rod less during the casting stroke. This can make some rods feel underlined and force the angler to quicken his or her stroke.

I tend to use whatever weight-forward line happens to be on my reel at the moment, without a great preference between traditional and textured lines. I buy whichever type I can acquire from one of the major manufacturers the cheapest and then spend as much time as possible fishing it to become fully accustomed to how it works with my rod and leader.

LEADERS AND TIPPET
In spite of what you may have read or been told, as long as you're using a trout leader produced by any of the major fly-fishing tackle companies or tied by someone who followed an established leader recipe, leaders have never been the reason you have failed to catch a fish. If you're good at fly fishing, nearly all mass-produced leaders will work fine. If you're not good, there's no magic leader formula that will compensate for a lack of casting and mending ability or a good understanding of which fly to tie to your leader.

Hand-Tied vs. Knotless
I prefer knotless leaders. People are often surprised to learn that I haven't hand-tied a leader in over 20 years. I certainly know how to do it—not knowing how to do something should never be the reason you don't do something in fly fishing. I just don't see any reason to do it. Time is precious, and there are many things I'd rather do than tie leaders. But fly fishing at its core should make you happy. And if tying leaders is your thing, then you should tie them. Lots of anglers do this, including some of the best fly fishers I know. Personally, I have never found an advantage in using hand-tied leaders.

Knots are just one more thing that can go wrong wherever you use them. So why would I want a string of knots on my leader? For some of my first-time fly-fishing guide clients, I don't even tie tippet to their leaders because I know they'll break it on a fish or by getting caught in a tree. When their leader gets too short, I put on a new one for them. You've spent all this money on tackle, gas, and everything else that encompasses fly fishing. Why skimp on a $4 leader?

Fluorocarbon vs. Nylon

For my own dry-fly fishing, I generally use a triple surgeon's knot to tie 2 to 3 feet of fluorocarbon tippet into my knotless leader, depending on the type of water I'm fishing. I use longer tippets for flatter water. The advantages and disadvantages of fluorocarbon have been debated for as long as the material has existed. It is more expensive than nylon (often called mono by anglers). Fluorocarbon absorbs water more quickly than nylon, and that makes it sink. I've read many times that fluorocarbon should not be used with dry flies because it will sink and submerge your fly. Some anglers also believe that the stiffness of fluorocarbon compared to nylon will make your flies drag more easily. But I have never found either of these things to be a problem. I also don't mind that the fluorocarbon sinks a little more than nylon. When the tippet tied to your dry fly rides on the water's surface, it casts a shadow more easily, and that could inhibit a trout from eating your fly.

The 6X fluorocarbon tied to this tiny CDC emerger didn't sink the fly, and it looked good enough for this rainbow to eat. The extra cost associated with fluorocarbon could make some anglers choose nylon tippets instead. But the myth that fluorocarbon sinks your dry flies shouldn't be part of your decision-making process.

I use fluorocarbon with my dry-fly rigs mostly because of its abrasion-resistance properties—fluorocarbon is purportedly more abrasion resistant than nylon and when fluorocarbon does abrade, it retains a higher breaking strength than abraded nylon. So if a trout rubs your tippet along a rock while you're fighting it, the fluorocarbon is supposed to be less likely to wear and to remain stronger even if it does. But some very knowledgeable anglers dispute this ability. I don't know for certain who's correct, but I've been successfully using fluorocarbon in conjunction with dry flies for a very long time.

If you decide to use fluorocarbon tippet attached to a nylon leader, you need to be aware that the stiffer fluorocarbon material will cut nylon in your knot if you do not take precautions. You should skip two sizes between the leader and tippet diameter—so 5X fluorocarbon tippet to 3X nylon leader, and so on. You don't need to worry about this if you're attaching fluorocarbon tippet to a fluorocarbon leader. But I don't usually use fluorocarbon leaders when dry-fly fishing because I've not found a distinct advantage to justify its substantial cost increase over nylon leaders.

Leader Length and Tippet Strength

I generally use the standard industry leader lengths of 7.5, 9, and 12 feet, but these lengths will vary if/when I add tippet. I only use the shortest (7.5-foot) leaders in two circumstances: if I am fishing a small, tree-lined stream with mostly broken water, or if I'm fishing large dry flies after dark. It's just easier to keep track of where my flies are going with a shorter leader.

The 9-foot length is probably the most common dry-fly leader used across the United States. Beginners sometimes struggle with this length and are better able to control a shorter leader. But for most anglers, 9 feet is the leader of choice, and it's the first leader length that you should strive to master. It is long enough to provide good separation from your fly line to your fly and yet short enough to remain manageable for most people if it's a little windy.

When I'm fishing flat water, whether in a midsize spring creek or a large tailwater river, I'll use 12-foot leaders. And if the fish are particularly wary, I'll tie 3 feet of tippet into it. This 15-foot leader configuration is generally the longest setup I'll use for dry-fly fishing. If you are new to dry-fly fishing, I would not advise using this leader configuration until you master the 9- and 12-foot lengths. Long leaders are difficult for many people to control, and if you throw a tailing loop or fail to turn the leader over because you are over- or underpowering your casting stroke, then you'll just end up with a frustrating mess. This will be compounded if it's windy or if you're trying to cast around obstructions like tree branches or other streamside vegetation. It's always better to cast a shorter leader that you can control rather than a longer one that causes you to struggle.

It's generally best to use the heaviest tippet that you can and still have the fish eat your fly. But be aware that many anglers struggle when changing tippet sizes often, never becoming fully acclimated to their individual breaking strengths. If you get accustomed to fishing only 4X tippet with large dry flies, you'll probably break fish off when you have to switch to 6X for smaller insects on calmer water. The type of water and size of the aquatic insects in the places you fish most often should determine the tippet strength you fish with the most. I almost never fished dry-fly tippet heavier than 6X when I lived in the East. But 4X and 5X are my most common diameters when imitating the large insects often found on the larger western waters. I have only one spool of 7X tippet in my pack, and I can't remember the last time I used it, even with tiny midges. Most of the time, if you improve your mending or casting angle to get a better drift, you won't have to use tippet so thin that it breaks easily or tires a fish to exhaustion as you land it.

ACCESSORIES TO KEEP YOUR FLIES FLOATING

There are some very important accessories that you should consider employing to get the most from your dry-fly fishing. From the moment you make

The protective slime that covers this rainbow trout's body will make the Adams Parachute dry fly in its mouth struggle to float for the next rising fish. After I catch a fish, I swish my dry fly in the water, then squeeze out the moisture with an amadou patch. I then brush it with a desiccant/floatant, and it's ready to go.

your first cast with a fresh dry fly, the world is conspiring against you to make it sink. Dry flies are formed on metal hooks—thinner, lighter wire than nymph hooks, but metal wire nonetheless. They incorporate materials that will eventually absorb water. And if you catch a fish on a dry fly, that fly will now absorb even more water as you fight the fish and be covered in fish slime when you land it.

There are a lot of floatant options on the market today. All of them will work well if you follow their directions, and none of them will work as well as you'd like. All fly anglers would be happy to treat our dry flies at home the night before a fishing trip with a waterproofing agent that makes them float like a cork until they fall to pieces after being eaten by a hundred huge trout. And though some companies have tried to manufacture this impossible product, no one has done it so far.

Most floatants are best used before a fly gets wet. So don't tie on a dry fly and throw it into the water while you search your pack for your floatant. I usually begin with a gel floatant like Gehrke's Gink or Loon's Aquel. Some anglers are insistent that Aquel works better than Gink because it doesn't liquefy during

warm weather. That really doesn't matter to me. Just don't squeeze the Gink bottle as hard when its warm or it will ooze out all over your hand. And make sure the lid is closed if you hang it upside down from your pack or it will be everywhere before you realize it. A lot of anglers use too much gel floatant on their flies and this can actually make them sink. Use the smallest amount possible and rub it into the fly to make sure all parts that are supposed to float have absorbed some floatant.

Drift boats can be great tools for your dry-fly fishing, as they help you reach fish you otherwise could not. But because you stand above the water to fish from a drift boat, the casting angles are different from when you're wading. It can take some fishermen a while to adjust.

You shouldn't use most gel floatants on dry flies that incorporate CDC feathers or snowshoe rabbit feet fur into their construction. The wispy CDC feathers, which are found near a gland on a duck's back end, float partially because they retain some of the gland's preen oil and also because their many barbs trap air bubbles. The snowshoe fur also aids floatation by trapping air bubbles. If you use a gel-based floatant, you'll mat these fibers and cause the flies to sink.

But there are products designed to help keep CDC and snowshoe flies afloat. Tiemco's Dry Magic is the one I prefer most. Price is its only drawback. One tube of Dry Magic will cost you nearly as much as three bottles of Gink. But then you are probably putting Dry Magic on a $3 fly tied to a $4 leader attached to a $100 fly line—you get the idea. The price is minimal compared to its ability to keep your dries floating; it works well.

Eventually, no matter what you dress your flies with before using them, they will begin to sink. The first thing I do when my fly sinks, even after false casting to help dry it, is to squeeze the water out. I keep an amadou patch for this within easy reach on the outside of my pack. Amadou comes from a fungus that grows on trees, and it's fairly rare and expensive. But it's fantastic for removing water from sinking dry flies. You can also buy a product called Samadou, which is a synthetic version of amadou, but I haven't found Samadou to work any better than using my shirt or any other dry fabric for expelling water from my dries. Don't waste your money.

After squeezing the water from my dry fly with the amadou, I dust it with a powder desiccant and floatant, usually Frog's Fanny, but there are several options available at most fly shops. You could just reapply gel floatant after the amadou, but I've found that using a desiccant/floatant makes the fly float higher, for a longer time period, after the fly becomes waterlogged. Just make sure that you blow off any of the residual powder from your fly; remember, the powder is pulling in moisture and it will actually make your fly sink if you leave it on there. Be careful opening the desiccant bottle in wind—some of it will blow away—and you'll already go through it quickly enough just by fishing. But I hope you have to replenish your desiccant often; it probably means you've been catching a lot of trout with dry flies.

SELECTED READING

Gentle currents, easy wading, good hatches, and lots of eager Yellowstone cutthroat trout combine to make the Lamar Valley in Yellowstone National Park a true dry-fly fisher's heaven.

Older books that helped me when I was learning to fish dry flies

Fox, Charles K. *Rising Trout*. Harrisburg, PA: Foxcrest, 1967.

Marinaro, Vincent C. *In the Ring of the Rise*. New York: Crown, 1976.

———. *A Modern Dry-Fly Code*. New York: G. P. Putnam's Sons, 1950.

Meck, Charles R. *Meeting and Fishing the Hatches*. New York: Winchester Press, 1977.

Casting and fishing books

Jaworowski, Ed. *The Cast*. Mechanicsburg, PA: Stackpole Books, 1992.

———. *Perfecting the Cast*. Lanham, MD: Stackpole Books, 2021.

Kreh, Lefty. *Casting with Lefty Kreh*. Mechanicsburg, PA: Stackpole Books, 2008.

Meck, Charles. *Fishing Tandem Flies*. Boiling Springs, PA: Headwater Books, 2007.

Books about specific eastern insects

Ames Jr., Thomas. *Caddisflies*. Mechanicsburg, PA: Stackpole Books, 2009.

Caucci, Al, and Bob Nastasi. *Hatches II*. Guilford, CT: Lyons Press, 2004.

LaFontaine, Gary. *Caddisflies*. Guilford, CT: Lyons Press, 1989.

Meck, Charles, and Paul Weamer. *Pocketguide to Pennsylvania Hatches*. New Cumberland, PA: Headwater Books, 2009.

Takahashi, Rick, and Jerry Hubka. *Modern Midges: Tying and Fishing the World's Most Effective Patterns*. New Cumberland, PA: Headwater Books, 2009.

Weamer, Paul. *The Bug Book*. Boiling Springs, PA: Headwater Books, 2016.

Weamer, Paul. *Pocketguide to New York Hatches*. Mechanicsburg, PA: Stackpole Books, 2013.

Books about specific western insects

Caucci, Al, and Bob Nastasi. *Hatches II*. Guilford, CT: Lyons Press, 2004.

Hafele, Rick, and Dave Hughes. *The Complete Book of Western Hatches*. Portland, OR: Frank Amato Publications, 1981.

Hughes, Dave. *Pocketguide to Western Hatches*. Mechanicsburg, PA: Stackpole Books, 2011.

LaFontaine, Gary. *Caddisflies*. Guilford, CT: Lyons Press, 1989.

Takahashi, Rick, and Jerry Hubka. *Modern Midges: Tying and Fishing the World's Most Effective Patterns*. New Cumberland, PA: Headwater Books, 2009.

Weamer, Paul. *The Bug Book*. Boiling Springs, PA: Headwater Books, 2016.

INDEX